901468

DATE DUE

DE 2 '90			
AP 15 '91	T.G		
OC 14 '91			
T.F			
JA 13 '92			
DE 21 '92			
NO 27 '93			
DE 5 '94			

901468

THE
NAVAJOS

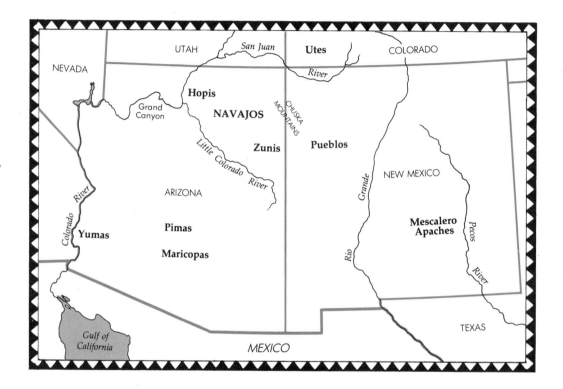

THE NAVAJOS

Peter Iverson
Arizona State University

Frank W. Porter III
General Editor

CHELSEA HOUSE PUBLISHERS
New York   Philadelphia

On the cover A silver bracelet set with five polished turquoise stones, made by Navajo artisan Juan Abata.

Chelsea House Publishers
Editor-in-Chief Nancy Toff
Executive Editor Remmel T. Nunn
Managing Editor Karyn Gullen Browne
Copy Chief Juliann Barbato
Picture Editor Adrian G. Allen
Art Director Maria Epes
Manufacturing Manager Gerald Levine

Indians of North America
Senior Editor Liz Sonneborn

Staff for **THE NAVAJOS**
Associate Editor Clifford W. Crouch
Copy Editor Philip Koslow
Editorial Assistant Judith D. Weinstein
Assistant Art Director Loraine Machlin
Designer Donna Sinisgalli
Design Assistant James Baker
Picture Researcher Sandy Jones
Production Manager Joseph Romano
Production Coordinator Marie Claire Cebrián

First Printing

1 3 5 7 9 8 6 4 2

Library of Congress Cataloging-in-Publication Data

Iverson, Peter.
The Navajos / Peter Iverson.
    p.   cm.—(Indians of North America)
Includes bibliographical references.
Summary: Examines the history, culture, changing fortunes, and current situation of the Navajo Indians.
ISBN 1-55546-719-9
      0-7910-0390-6 (pbk.)
1. Navajo Indians.   [1. Navajo Indians.   2. Indians of North America.] I. Title. II. Series: Indians of North America (Chelsea House Publishers)   89-36621
E99.N3I89   1990   CIP
973'.04972—dc20   AC

CONTENTS

Indians of North America:
Conflict and Survival   7
by Frank W. Porter III

1. Into the Fourth World   13
2. The Evolution of Navajo Culture   27
3. The Long Walk   39
4. The Weaving Together of a People   49
5. The Time of Livestock Reduction   59
   Picture Essay
   From Silver and Wool   65
6. The Modern Navajo Era Begins   79
7. The Navajo Nation   89

   Bibliography   104
   The Navajos at a Glance   105
   Glossary   106
   Index   108

INDIANS OF NORTH AMERICA

The Abenaki

American Indian
  Literature

The Apache

The Arapaho

The Archaeology
  of North America

The Aztecs

The Cahuilla

The Catawbas

The Cherokee

The Cheyenne

The Chickasaw

The Chinook

The Chipewyan

The Choctaw

The Chumash

The Coast Salish Peoples

The Comanche

The Creeks

The Crow

The Eskimo

Federal Indian Policy

The Hidatsa

The Huron

The Iroquois

The Kiowa

The Kwakiutl

The Lenapes

The Lumbee

The Maya

The Menominee

The Modoc

The Montagnais-Naskapi

The Nanticoke

The Narragansett

The Navajos

The Nez Perce

The Ojibwa

The Osage

The Paiute

The Pima-Maricopa

The Potawatomi

The Powhatan Tribes

The Pueblo

The Quapaws

The Seminole

The Tarahumara

The Tunica-Biloxi

Urban Indians

The Wampanoag

Women in American
  Indian Society

The Yakima

The Yankton Sioux

The Yuma

CHELSEA HOUSE PUBLISHERS

INDIANS OF NORTH AMERICA: CONFLICT AND SURVIVAL

Frank W. Porter III

The Indians survived our open intention of wiping them out, and since the tide turned they have even weathered our good intentions toward them, which can be much more deadly.

John Steinbeck
America and Americans

When Europeans first reached the North American continent, they found hundreds of tribes occupying a vast and rich country. The newcomers quickly recognized the wealth of natural resources. They were not, however, so quick or willing to recognize the spiritual, cultural, and intellectual riches of the people they called Indians.

The Indians of North America examines the problems that develop when people with different cultures come together. For American Indians, the consequences of their interaction with non-Indian people have been both productive and tragic. The Europeans believed they had "discovered" a "New World," but their religious bigotry, cultural bias, and materialistic world view kept them from appreciating and understanding the people who lived in it. All too often they attempted to change the way of life of the indigenous people. The Spanish conquistadores wanted the Indians as a source of labor. The Christian missionaries, many of whom were English, viewed them as potential converts. French traders and trappers used the Indians as a means to obtain pelts. As Francis Parkman, the 19th-century historian, stated, "Spanish civilization crushed the Indian; English civilization scorned and neglected him; French civilization embraced and cherished him."

7

Nearly 500 years later, many people think of American Indians as curious vestiges of a distant past, waging a futile war to survive in a Space Age society. Even today, our understanding of the history and culture of American Indians is too often derived from unsympathetic, culturally biased, and inaccurate reports. The American Indian, described and portrayed in thousands of movies, television programs, books, articles, and government studies, has either been raised to the status of the "noble savage" or disparaged as the "wild Indian" who resisted the westward expansion of the American frontier.

Where in this popular view are the real Indians, the human beings and communities whose ancestors can be traced back to ice-age hunters? Where are the creative and indomitable people whose sophisticated technologies used the natural resources to ensure their survival, whose military skill might even have prevented European settlement of North America if not for devastating epidemics and disruption of the ecology? Where are the men and women who are today diligently struggling to assert their legal rights and express once again the value of their heritage?

The various Indian tribes of North America, like people everywhere, have a history that includes population expansion, adaptation to a range of regional environments, trade across wide networks, internal strife, and warfare. This was the reality. Europeans justified their conquests, however, by creating a mythical image of the New World and its native people. In this myth, the New World was a virgin land, waiting for the Europeans. The arrival of Christopher Columbus ended a timeless primitiveness for the original inhabitants.

Also part of this myth was the debate over the origins of the American Indians. Fantastic and diverse answers were proposed by the early explorers, missionairies, and settlers. Some thought that the Indians were descended from the Ten Lost Tribes of Israel, others that they were descended from inhabitants of the lost continent of Atlantis. One writer suggested that the Indians had reached North America in another Noah's ark.

A later myth, perpetrated by many historians, focused on the relentless persecution during the past five centuries until only a scattering of these "primitive" people remained to be herded onto reservations. This view fails to chronicle the overt and covert ways in which the Indians successfully coped with the intruders.

All of these myths presented one-sided interpretations that ignored the complexity of European and American events and policies. All left serious questions unanswered. What were the origins of the American Indians? Where did they come from? How and when did they get to the New World? What was their life—their culture—really like?

In the late 1800s, anthropologists and archaeologists in the Smithsonian Institution's newly created Bureau of American Ethnology in Washington,

D.C., began to study scientifically the history and culture of the Indians of North America. They were motivated by an honest belief that the Indians were on the verge of extinction and that along with them would vanish their languages, religious beliefs, technology, myths, and legends. These men and women went out to visit, study, and record data from as many Indian communities as possible before this information was forever lost.

By this time there was a new myth in the national consciousness. American Indians existed as figures in the American past. They had performed a historical mission. They had challenged white settlers who trekked across the continent. Once conquered, however, they were supposed to accept graciously the way of life of their conquerors.

The reality again was different. American Indians resisted both actively and passively. They refused to lose their unique identity, to be assimilated into white society. Many whites viewed the Indians not only as members of a conquered nation but also as "inferior" and "unequal." The rights of the Indians could be expanded, contracted, or modified as the conquerors saw fit. In every generation, white society asked itself what to do with the American Indians. Their answers have resulted in the twists and turns of federal Indian policy.

There were two general approaches. One way was to raise the Indians to a "higher level" by "civilizing" them. Zealous missionaries considered it their Christian duty to elevate the Indian through conversion and scanty education. The other approach was to ignore the Indians until they disappeared under pressure from the ever-expanding white society. The myth of the "vanishing Indian" gave stronger support to the latter option, helping to justify the taking of the Indians' land.

Prior to the end of the 18th century, there was no national policy on Indians simply because the American nation had not yet come into existence. American Indians similarly did not possess a political or social unity with which to confront the various Europeans. They were not homogeneous. Rather, they were loosely formed bands and tribes, speaking nearly 300 languages and thousands of dialects. The collective identity felt by Indians today is a result of their common experiences of defeat and/or mistreatment at the hands of whites.

During the colonial period, the British crown did not have a coordinated policy toward the Indians of North America. Specific tribes (most notably the Iroquois and the Cherokee) became military and political pawns used by both the crown and the individual colonies. The success of the American Revolution brought no immediate change. When the United States acquired new territory from France and Mexico in the early 19th century, the federal government wanted to open this land to settlement by homesteaders. But the Indian tribes that lived on this land had signed treaties with European governments assuring their title to the land. Now the United States assumed legal responsibility for honoring these treaties.

At first, President Thomas Jefferson believed that the Louisiana Purchase contained sufficient land for both the Indians and the white population. Within a generation, though, it became clear that the Indians would not be allowed to remain. In the 1830s the federal government began to coerce the eastern tribes to sign treaties agreeing to relinquish their ancestral land and move west of the Mississippi River. Whenever these negotiations failed, President Andrew Jackson used the military to remove the Indians. The southeastern tribes, promised food and transportation during their removal to the West, were instead forced to walk the "Trail of Tears." More than 4,000 men, woman, and children died during this forced march. The "removal policy" was successful in opening the land to homesteaders, but it created enormous hardships for the Indians.

By 1871 most of the tribes in the United States had signed treaties ceding most or all of their ancestral land in exchange for reservations and welfare. The treaty terms were intended to bind both parties for all time. But in the General Allotment Act of 1887, the federal government changed its policy again. Now the goal was to make tribal members into individual landowners and farmers, encouraging their absorption into white society. This policy was advantageous to whites who were eager to acquire Indian land, but it proved disastrous for the Indians. One hundred thirty-eight million acres of reservation land were subdivided into tracts of 160, 80, or as little as 40 acres, and allotted tribe members on an individual basis. Land owned in this way was said to have "trust status" and could not be sold. But the surplus land—all Indian land not allotted to individuals—was opened (for sale) to white settlers. Ultimately, more than 90 million acres of land were taken from the Indians by legal and illegal means.

The resulting loss of land was a catastrophe for the Indians. It was necessary to make it illegal for Indians to sell their land to non-Indians. The Indian Reorganization Act of 1934 officially ended the allotment period. Tribes that voted to accept the provisions of this act were reorganized, and an effort was made to purchase land within preexisting reservations to restore an adequate land base.

Ten years later, in 1944, federal Indian policy again shifted. Now the federal government wanted to get out of the "Indian business." In 1953 an act of Congress named specific tribes whose trust status was to be ended "at the earliest possible time." This new law enabled the United States to end unilaterally, whether the Indians wished it or not, the special status that protected the land in Indian tribal reservations. In the 1950s federal Indian policy was to transfer federal responsibility and jurisdiction to state governments, encourage the physical relocation of Indian peoples from reservations to urban areas, and hasten the termination, or extinction, of tribes.

Between 1954 and 1962 Congress passed specific laws authorizing the termination of more than 100 tribal groups. The stated purpose of the termination policy was to ensure the full and complete integration of Indians into American society. However, there is a less benign way to interpret this legislation. Even as termination was being discussed in Congress, 133 separate bills were introduced to permit the transfer of trust land ownership from Indians to non-Indians.

With the Johnson administration in the 1960s the federal government began to reject termination. In the 1970s yet another Indian policy emerged. Known as "self-determination," it favored keeping the protective role of the federal government while increasing tribal participation in, and control of, important areas of local government. In 1983 President Reagan, in a policy statement on Indian affairs, restated the unique "government is government" relationship of the United States with the Indians. However, federal programs since then have moved toward transferring Indian affairs to individual states, which have long desired to gain control of Indian land and resources.

As long as American Indians retain power, land, and resources that are coveted by the states and the federal government, there will continue to be a "clash of cultures," and the issues will be contested in the courts, Congress, the White House, and even in the international human rights community. To give all Americans a greater comprehension of the issues and conflicts involving American Indians today is a major goal of this series. These issues are not easily understood, nor can these conflicts be readily resolved. The study of North American Indian history and culture is a necessary and important step toward that comprehension. All Americans must learn the history of the relations between the Indians and the federal government, recognize the unique legal status of the Indians, and understand the heritage and cultures of the Indians of North America.

The Fourth World, *by Navajo artist Andy Tsinajinnie. According to the Navajos' origin story, all creatures journeyed through three lower worlds before they came to live on earth.*

1

INTO THE
FOURTH WORLD

Peoples all over the world tell stories about their beginnings. By repeating tales passed down by previous generations, a society's storytellers pass along a heritage as old as memory and as new as the youngest child within the community. The stories not only entertain, they instruct. They reinforce in the listeners a sense of the right way of doing things, the right way of behaving as a member of their society.

Good storytellers are like weavers. They gather together the various strands of a people's past and from them create patterns forming a complex but ultimately unified design. Different weavers fashion different styles of rugs. Yet, to the discerning eye, there can be no question about what kind of weaver made any particular rug. There may be imitations; there may be fakes. But a real Navajo rug—for the Navajo people are in fact renowned as master weavers—is one that cannot be mistaken. And a good Navajo rug, like the Navajo stories, like the people themselves, will last.

The Navajos are today the largest Indian tribe in North America. Their homeland occupies much of northeastern Arizona and portions of New Mexico and Utah. Yet they have not always been a large group, nor have they always lived in their current location. The Navajos' history is a story of both change and continuity. Their ancient tales help to explain who they have been and who they are now.

The Navajos' own story of their origin begins with a description of the emergence of all living things through a series of worlds. Some storytellers say the first world was black, the second blue, the third yellow, and call the fourth—the present world—glittering or bright. Others speak of fewer or more worlds. But all the stories in some way emphasize the number four. Four is an important number for the Navajos, as it is for many other Indian groups. It reminds the Navajos of the four seasons, the four directions, the four sacred mountains of their territory, and other important aspects of tribal life.

The Navajos' emergence story provides its hearers with several lessons to guide them in life. The importance of harmony within a group of people is particularly stressed. In most versions, the main reason humans and other creatures have to move from one world to the next is that they cannot get along with one another. In one variation, men and women quarrel over a misunderstanding. The two groups then separate, but they do not prosper in each other's absence. Eventually the men and women reunite and thereafter have a better appreciation of the need to try to understand and tolerate the ways of the opposite sex.

In all four worlds, humans coexist with insects and animals. These include squirrels, turkeys, lizards, and deer—creatures familiar to the Navajos of today. These animals' presence during the emergence journey implies that people are not superior to, or meant to live independent of, other forms of life.

The animals in the Navajos' origin story have particular characteristics.

The most prominent example is Coyote. Coyote is a trickster and a joker whose antics inevitably result in problems for others. Coyote plays a similar role in the Navajos' many stories about him in this world.

When all beings finally emerge into the present world, they find that it is covered entirely with water. They manage, however, to come to terms with a monster who controls the waters, so that eventually the waters withdraw and the world known to the Navajos today begins to form. The four sacred mountains that mark the traditional boundaries of Navajo country take shape: San Francisco Peak (also known as Abalone Shell Mountain) in the west, Blanca Peak (Dawn or White Shell Mountain) in the east, Mount Taylor (Blue Bead or Turquoise Mountain) in the south, and La Plata Mountain (Obsidian Mountain) in the north.

As the story is commonly told, it is at this time that the sun, moon, and stars first appear in the sky, day and night come to be, and the year divides into seasons. This is also the period during which the First Man and the First Woman arrive in the vicinity of what is now called Huerfano Mountain in New Mexico. A baby is then born of the mingling of darkness and dawn at Gobernador Knob, a geologic formation in northeastern New Mexico. First Man and First Woman find the baby after they hear her cry one morning at dawn. Together, they rear the infant with the aid of instructions from sacred spirits known as the Holy People. The child grows up to be Changing Woman, who is said to have arrived in the Navajo world at this time because only then was it ready for her. With the four sacred mountains and all plants and animals in their proper places, the world has achieved a kind of beauty and harmony, which, the storytellers note, is the opposite of the chaos found in the previous worlds.

When Changing Woman reaches puberty, the Holy People conduct a ceremony for her so that she may walk in beauty as an adult. This ritual, called the *kinaalda*, is still performed for young Navajo women. This is another example of how the origin story explains elements of contemporary Navajo life.

Later in the story, Changing Woman falls asleep by a waterfall, where she is visited by the Sun. She then becomes pregnant and gives birth to twin sons. She names one Child Born of Water and the other Monster Slayer.

A 1914 photograph of two Navajo men talking. Tribal myths such as the origin story were passed down orally from one generation to the next for centuries.

Sun God and His Wife, *painted by Navajo artist Gerald Nailor in 1938. Nailor's work depicts the Sun visiting Changing Woman, who, according to Navajo oral tradition, created the Navajo people from a mixture of cornmeal and scrapings of her own skin.*

The two boys grow hardy by getting up before sunrise and running and by rolling in the snow. They also learn to hunt. During their childhood, Changing Woman creates the corn plant. Later, she mixes cornmeal with scrapings of her own skin to create the first Navajo people.

While hunting one day, Changing Woman's two sons see a small hole in the ground. A voice coming from the hole urges them to go inside it. The hole magically grows wider, and they descend into it, using a ladder they find awaiting them. Inside, they meet another legendary figure of the Navajo people, Spider Woman. (Later, she will teach the Navajos how to weave.)

The boys ask Spider Woman who their father is, because their mother has always refused to tell them. Spider Woman says only that she knows his identity and will assist them in finding him. She also explains to them that their father could help them destroy the monsters who have been plaguing all people on earth. But before they can reach their father, the boys will have to undergo a long, difficult, and dangerous journey.

Because Child Born of Water and Monster Slayer have grown strong through proper living, they are well prepared for their ordeal. Yet they cannot reach the Sun unaided. In order to survive the journey, they learn from Spider Woman about the obstacles that await them. She teaches the twins special prayers and explains to them carefully what they will encounter and how to prevent disaster. To see their father, Monster Slayer and Child Born of Water will have to avoid or overcome four hazards on their way to the Sun's residence, then maneuver past four more hazards guarding his domain.

Armed with this knowledge, the boys are able to get by the reeds that cut the unwary traveler and cause him to bleed to death. They successfully cross the sands that can shift and smother a wanderer. They barely elude being crushed by a canyon that threatens to close in on all who pass through it. Finally, by taking an alternate route to the south, they bypass four rock columns that have the power to turn them into withered old men.

Before the twins reach the Sun's home, they enlist the assistance of a worm and a water bug to transport them across a bog and an ocean. Monster Slayer and Child Born of Water then come to the obstacles guarding the Sun's residence—the great snake, the enormous black bear, the big thunder, and the big wind. By chanting the prayers Spider Woman taught them, the twins safely gain entrance.

Suddenly faced by the twins, the Sun refuses to accept that they are his children. He says he cannot be their father, in part because he does not want his wife to know that he might have impregnated another woman. The Sun tells the boys he will believe they are his sons only if they go through still another series of dangerous physical ordeals.

After the twins manage to survive these, the Sun, true to his word, admits that he is their father. To reward them for passing his tests, the Sun offers the boys wonderful things—including corn, horses, and jewels—from the four rooms of his house. But Child Born of Water and Monster Slayer say they want only his help in killing the monsters. The Sun then gives them each a particular type of lightning to use to destroy their enemies and flint armor to wear for protection.

The Navajos tell many stories of the great adventures the twins had as they sought to slaughter the monsters. For example, in one tale they kill an incredible giant. When the giant falls, he bleeds profusely. The black lava flow near present-day Grants, New Mexico, is said to be the giant's dried blood. The twins also shoot and kill a monstrous bird that had resided on top of another Navajo country landmark—an isolated mountain in northwestern New Mexico known as Shiprock. Tellers of these stories explain that the world became safe for the Navajo people to inhabit because of the brothers' heroism. But they also remind their listeners that the twins triumphed only because they were given help from many others, including Spider Woman, the Sun, and such seemingly insignificant creatures as the worm and the water bug.

The Navajos' stories about their origins emphasize that the people's association with their current surroundings dates back to the very beginnings of humankind. But the passages from one world to the next and the many journeys, trials, and adventures described in the various tales may also be seen as the story of an extended migration. Interpreted in this way, the tales are like a mythic mirror of the Navajos' own early history, based on what archaeologists and linguists have concluded about how the tribe came to inhabit what is now the southwestern United States.

Archaeologists are scientists who study the past as revealed by the objects left behind by past societies. Many archaeologists believe that North and South America were populated by the descendants of people who thousands of years ago migrated from Asia across the Bering Strait into what is now Alaska. Over time, humans gradually wandered southward, and eventually they inhabited lands throughout the two continents.

Archaeologists also believe that the Navajo people lived for a very long time in far northern North America. In their judgment, 2,000 years ago the Navajos still resided in what is now northwestern Canada or Alaska.

By about 500 years ago the Navajos had probably become residents of the Southwest. The exact route the Navajos took to their new home and the precise date of their arrival there remain subject to debate. However, linguists (scholars of human languages) have a theory about the tribe's migration. They classify the Navajo language as part of a group of related languages known as the Athapaskan family. (Athapaska is a lake in northwestern Canada.) Other Athapaskan languages include those spoken by Indian groups who today live in the subarctic, as well as those spoken by some other peoples, such as the Hupa, who inhabit various locations scattered between there and the Southwest. Of the many Indian tribes now living in the Southwest, only the Apaches are related linguistically to the Navajos. Therefore, linguists argue that the Apaches and the Navajos were once a single group and probably did not separate until after they had come to their present location. In fact, the Navajos' name is a shortened form of the original Spanish name for them, Apaches de Nabajó (Apaches of the Nabajó). The word *Nabajó* may originally

Shiprock, a geological formation in northwestern New Mexico, in a 1914 photograph. The Navajos' stories associate Shiprock and other landmarks of the tribe's homeland with the beginnings of mankind.

have been a place name or may have been an Indian term meaning "planted fields."

People who move bring with them their culture—that is, their society's way of life, with its own special beliefs, rituals, behavior patterns, and means of survival. These traditions influence the choices they make about how they lead their new lives. This abstract cargo, often referred to as "cultural baggage," is as important to immigrants' survival as the physical possessions they pack. But once they arrive at their destination, they face decisions, often difficult ones, about which elements of this baggage they must discard and which they may profitably keep. The Navajos retained one of the most central elements of their cultural baggage—their language—when they came to their new home. They might conceivably have

A woman weaving a basket, photographed in 1954. Basketmaking was one of the traditions the early Navajos continued to practice after they migrated from what is now northern Canada to the southwestern United States.

adopted another language, just as immigrants to the United States today often learn English. But when the Navajos arrived in the Southwest, no one language dominated the region, for there were relatively few people and no single controlling group in the area. It is not surprising that, given no compelling reason to change, they kept their language.

In other matters, the Navajos faced more complicated choices. Today technology sometimes allows people to maintain a certain way of life even in a normally hostile environment. For example, people from Ohio who move to the desert land of southern Arizona can maintain a grassy lawn through irrigation. But the Navajos of 500 years ago did not have the luxury of such technology. When they moved to an environment radically different from that of northern North America, they had to confront without buffers the dilemma of change. Although they had probably been able to maintain most elements of their old culture during their long migration south, they had to decide how best to adapt to the world they encountered once they arrived in their new home.

In the northern regions, the Navajos had obtained food by hunting wild game, fishing, and gathering wild plants. They had made bows and arrows and harpoons to kill their prey. The Navajos also built wooden enclosures, into which they drove large game, such as elk and caribou, so that the trapped animals could be slaughtered more easily. They made clothing and cone-shaped houses from the skins of the animals they hunted. As they moved from place to place in search of game and wild vegetation, they wore snowshoes and used tame dogs to haul their goods on sleds. Although they did not make pottery, they did make baskets from tree bark. Usually they lived in small, loosely organized groups that anthropologists call bands. Their religious leaders were charged with the responsibility of mediating with the forces of nature and curing the sick.

Some aspects of this way of life transferred satisfactorily to the high desert country of the Southwest. But fishing and hunting many species of animals became less important because some fish and game were not plentiful in the Navajos' new home. New forms of transportation had to be developed that were appropriate to the rugged terrain. New clothing suitable for a hotter, drier climate had to be fashioned from available materials. Eventually, new types of dwellings were also devised.

Of course, these transformations did not occur overnight or in a season or even over a generation. But as the Navajos' migration over thousands of miles had already demonstrated, they were willing to accept change if necessary. Perhaps the most crucial adaptations the Navajos were forced to make were in their system of beliefs. Like most peoples all over the world, they had considered particular geographical features in their northern home to be sacred places. Certain mountains, valleys, and lakes, therefore, were firmly linked to their concept of the meaning of their lives. After they arrived in the Southwest, the Navajos had to come to terms with nothing less than a new earth and a new sky. This meant that they also had to redefine their ideas about who they were.

The Navajos responded by literally creating the world anew. With their origin story, they invested sacred significance in the majestic mountains they found in the Southwest. They identified specific places as the locations of events—such as the birth of Changing Woman—that had great importance to them as a people. Through this gradual process, the Navajos in effect said to their children: This is where we belong and where we will remain.

The Navajos did not have to evaluate and adjust their old culture in complete isolation, however, because when they came to the Southwest they did not come to an unpopulated land. Some Indian peoples had already lived there for centuries. Given the Navajos' adaptability, they were willing to learn from others, selectively adopting features of other societies that they found attractive or useful. Through this process, they could take something into their culture and in the course of many years make it Navajo. This cultural flexibility allowed them to prosper.

Initially the Navajos probably were most influenced by the people living closest to them. These people, today known as the Pueblos, lived in many independent villages along the Rio Grande in what is now northern New Mexico as well as in several isolated locations on the Colorado Plateau. Having migrated into the region from a northeastern direction, the Navajos first came into contact with the Pueblo people in what is now northwestern New Mexico. The Navajos, who call themselves Diné (the People), still call this region Dinétah (the Land of the People).

Some of the Pueblos had arrived in the Southwest as early as 900 years before the Navajos. By the time of the Navajo migration, these Pueblos had already come to terms with the land and had even learned to thrive in this arid and craggy environment. The Pueblos were good farmers. Although the Navajos probably had some contact with agricultural communities while traveling to the Southwest, they must have been impressed with the Pueblos' ability to grow corn, melons, and other crops. Over the years, the Pueblos had become so familiar with the terrain, climate, and seasonal changes that they were adept at farming using little water.

The Pueblo farmers' reliable source of food must have been esteemed tremendously by the Navajos, who in the north had had to travel constantly in search of animals to hunt and wild plants to gather. A successful farming community offers its inhabitants security and stability. Most important, it provides freedom from the fear of starvation, perhaps the greatest of all fears. It also allows a people to stay in one place for a long period of time.

In addition to the Pueblos, the Navajo people also came into contact with the Hopi Indians, living in what is now northern Arizona. But as fortune and fate would have it, the Hopis and other Pueblo Indian communities were soon not the only source for additions to the Navajos' culture. Not long after the Navajos arrived in their new home, people from another society on the other side of the world began to have an influence in the Southwest. In far-off Spain, business interests, curiosity about the distant country of Cathay (China), and improvements in sailing vessels all combined to encourage an era of exploration. By the end of the 1400s, Spain's queen, Isabella I, gave the Italian explorer Christopher Columbus the financial backing he needed to search for a new trade route to China. But Columbus's ships accidentally sailed instead to a world new to him and all other Europeans. The lives of all the native peoples of North and South America would be permanently altered.

After Columbus's voyage, the Spanish became the first great European colonizers by promptly dispatching explorers, traders, settlers, and missionaries to what is now Mexico, South America, and the western United States. Of course, not all Spanish colonists had exactly the same objectives, and their actions and priorities were not the same in all areas. Nonetheless, they all brought their own cultural baggage to their new home, which they called New Spain. This included their own language, religion (Christianity), dress, housing, and system of government. Even when the colonists confronted Indian societies, many Spaniards tended to think that they were moving into a world where no culture existed. To them, people who did not worship God through the Catholic church, speak Spanish, wear European-style clothing, observe the practice of church-sanctioned marriage, and live in European-style housing could not be considered civilized.

Spanish colonists had the most immediate impact on Indian groups that had well-established settlements, such as the Pueblos. Populous Pueblo villages proved to be prime sites for the establishment of missions by Spanish priests who came to the Southwest to convert the Indians to Christianity. But those Indian peoples, including the Navajos, who ranged over a wide territory, felt the Spanish presence only fitfully. For instance, if a Spanish missionary tried to compel a Navajo to at-

A Pueblo village in present-day Oraibi, Arizona. Long before the Navajos arrived in the Southwest, the Pueblo Indians had developed housing styles and farming methods that were well suited to the region's harsh climate.

tend mass, the Navajo could simply travel to a remote area of the tribe's lands to avoid the service.

Although few Navajos went to mass or learned to speak Spanish fluently, the tribe did choose to incorporate some elements of Spanish culture into its own. Along with their religious teachings, the missionaries brought European fruits and vegetables—such as peaches, potatoes, and wheat—and the knowledge of how to grow them. Span-

iards also introduced to the region cattle, sheep, and horses, all of which would become very important to the Navajos. Indeed, the raising of sheep became central to the Navajo way of life. Today it is difficult to imagine the Navajos living without large herds of sheep.

Ironically, the Spanish, who eventually destroyed the culture of many Indian groups in their conquest of North and South America, provided the Na-

This detail of a Navajo rock painting, which probably dates from the early 1800s, depicts Spaniards on horseback. The tribe first acquired horses, sheep, and cattle during the 17th century from Spanish colonists.

A shepherd and his flock, photographed in the 1970s. Raising sheep has been a central part of the Navajo way of life for centuries.

vajos with some of the key elements of their cultural identity. These very additions to the tribe's culture enabled it to become a major force in the Southwest. In 1492, when Columbus first crossed the Atlantic Ocean, few if any of the people of the region could have predicted that the immigrant Navajos would emerge as such an important Indian group. But the culture of New Spain, like the offspring of darkness and dawn, helped make the Navajo people's emergence into this new world possible. ▲

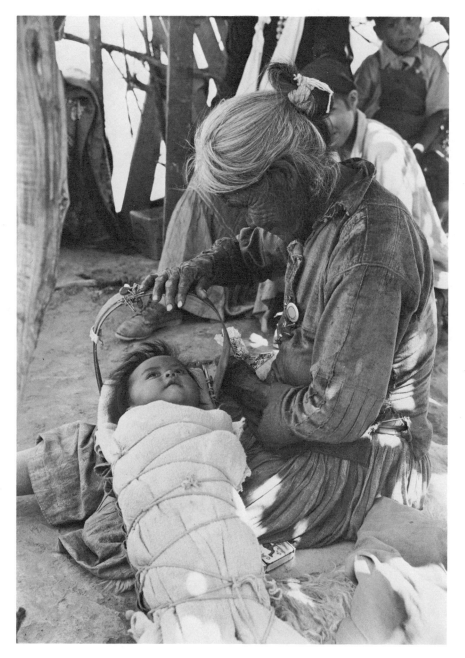

A Navajo woman looking after her grandchild. Navajo children learn what it means to be a member of the tribe by watching and imitating adults.

THE EVOLUTION
OF
NAVAJO CULTURE

The Navajos are often called a tribe—a term that is usually used to describe a group of individuals who are politically and economically united. The Navajos, however, did not become a cohesive people until the mid-19th century, more than two centuries after their first contact with the Spanish. During this 200-year period, most of the distinguishing features of their culture—those now considered distinctly Navajo—evolved. Some attributes of Navajo culture are easily perceived, such as the objects and animals the Navajos found to be of enduring value to them as a people. Other attributes are abstract and invisible but no less important. These include the beliefs, ceremonies, and social relationships that bound all Navajos to their community and imposed order, meaning, and purpose on their existence.

At birth, Navajo children became valued members of both their family and the larger community. Navajo parents placed their babies in cradleboards, beds made of a wooden platform and leather straps that were tied around the infants to keep them securely contained. Strapped in cradleboards, babies could be carried easily by their parents as they performed their daily activities. From this niche, infants watched the members of their family and learned how they lived and worked together. In time, young children came to realize that they belonged to this group and were expected eventually to contribute to its well-being. In Navajo society, the individual did matter, but primarily as a part of a larger social unit.

Navajo children were raised by the members of an extended family. Grandparents, aunts, uncles, and older siblings all played roles in a child's upbringing. Boys learned skills such as hunting, tracking, and ceremonial activities, and girls became adept at cooking, weaving, and similar domestic duties. Young Navajos were expected to learn from and emulate their elders. Both girls and boys, therefore, did not have to look far for role models for the responsibilities and privileges they would assume or enjoy later in life. Although children came to understand that living meant coping with change, they could also depend on a certain amount of continuity in their world.

Early in life, Navajo children learned that people rose before the sun. Their first glimpse of the new day was usually from their house, now called a hogan. In the subarctic, the early Navajos had used a pole or forked stick to prop up their hide-covered dwellings. In the Southwest, similarly, they used a pole or stick to help bolster a new kind of dwelling that they built primarily from earth. Over the generations, hogan builders came to use logs and strips of bark to create a cone- or dome-shaped skeleton that they covered with a thick coat of mud. A hole was left in the dwelling's wall to function as a doorway. These entrances always faced east, thus paying respect to the rising sun.

Each hogan had only a single room, which measured somewhere between 20 and 30 feet in diameter. The Navajos spent much of their time outdoors, but the unpredictable and sometimes harsh climate of the Southwest often forced them to stay within their hogans for extended periods of time. Because family members of all ages shared this small space, they all had to be careful to pick up after themselves, keep their own possessions (such as clothes and hunting equipment) in order, and observe and respect the needs of others. Families developed a strategy for where things belonged both within their hogan and in the area immediately around it. During the summer and early autumn, clothing, blankets, and items for cooking were kept outside and brought inside only as needed.

Although the Navajos, unlike the Pueblos, did not live in villages, people generally found it convenient to build their homes near their relatives. With this arrangement, the members of an extended family could work together to raise crops and livestock.

A young woman usually wed soon after reaching puberty. A marriage was commonly arranged by a woman's family and that of her prospective husband, who was often somewhat older than the bride-to-be. Because marriage was usually a lifelong proposition, families took the matter very seriously and discussed it among themselves. Although the practice was not common, an older man who had accumulated some wealth might have more than one wife. Because the family relationship played a large role in most marriages, a widow might also marry her deceased husband's brother.

Young married couples usually went to live in the vicinity of the wife's mother. This woman or another female elder set the rules of behavior for the individuals living in a cluster of hogans. She served as the center of a world in miniature, one that included a herd of sheep, the land used by the people of the group, their homes, and perhaps fields of corn and other vegetables or fruits, which were cared for by both men and women.

In this close-knit group, everyone— children and adults—had to mind how they acted because if a person misbehaved, it reflected badly on both them and their kin. A Navajo saying that is probably hundreds of years old describes someone who behaves inappropriately as acting as though he does not have any relatives.

All Navajos also belonged to a clan, a larger group of relatives who believed that they had descended from a common ancestor. Husbands and wives always belonged to different clans because fellow clan members were considered to be too closely related to produce healthy children.

Navajo society is today divided into about 60 clans, the members of which are scattered throughout the millions of acres the Navajos now call home. These clans include Todichi'iinii (Bitter Water), Ashiihi (Salt People), To'aheedliinii (Water Flowing Together), Kinyaa'aanii (Towering House People), and Tl'izilani (Many Goats). The name Tl'izilani indicates that some new clans came into existence over

A Navajo family outside their house, or hogan, *in 1914.*

time, because the Navajos had goats only after the arrival of the Spanish in the 1500s.

Navajo children were born into their mother's clan—a system of descent known as matrilineal—but they also felt a special bond to the members of their father's clan. The tie between a mother and her children, however, was the deepest and most significant of any bond between relatives in Navajo society.

Given the importance of the mother-child tie and the likelihood that a married couple would live near the woman's mother, a Navajo husband and his mother-in-law often had a tense relationship. The Navajos found a fairly effective means to deal with this problem:

A man usually tried never to speak to or even look at his wife's mother. Although this behavior did not entirely eliminate all confrontations, it did tend to make them less common and less serious.

By the late 1700s, the Navajo way of life revolved around the tribe's sheep herds. Their sheep were grazed in common but were owned by individual Navajos, who sometimes earmarked their animals and often knew them simply by sight. Most men and women owned at least a few, so virtually everyone had a direct interest in the herds' well-being. Parents gave their children lambs to look after and explained that these young sheep represented the beginning of the flock they would own as

A 1915 photograph of a girl watching a flock of sheep. Navajo parents gave lambs to their children to help them learn how to care for the animals.

adults. By caring for these animals, children became working, integral members of the larger community very early in life.

Sheep served many purposes. Once a year, in the spring, men and women used knives to shear the sheep of their wool. The wool was traditionally used by Navajo women to weave blankets. After the arrival of European traders, Navajo women commonly wore dresses of woven cloth. By the late 1800s, Navajo blankets and rugs had become vital items of trade and sale in the tribal economy. But long before that time, Navajo weavers made blankets for their family members. As the Navajos became familiar with the natural resources of the Southwest, they discovered plants, shrubs, trees, and cacti that yielded dyes that could be used to color spun wool. They soon learned how to weave the dyed wool to create bold designs.

Sheep were also a source of meat—both lamb (from a young animal) and mutton (from an adult sheep). Mutton was frequently the tougher and less tasty of the two. However, its flavor was often improved by combining it with vegetables, such as potatoes, and other ingredients to make a stew. They might eat this stew with frybread made with flour from their wheat harvest.

Navajos fed their sheep not only to their immediate family but also on occasion to other tribe members. The tribe placed a great value on generosity and on paying back the generous acts of others. It was therefore crucial for a person

A woman weaving a blanket on a large vertical loom in 1915. Traditionally, Navajo weavers made blankets for their family's use, but in the late 19th century they began to weave rugs for sale to non-Indians.

to be able to feed visiting clan members. Having enough extra meat to serve guests was also evidence of an individual's ability to tend his or her flock.

Meat from sheep was eaten at religious functions as well. Either alive or butchered, these animals often served as payment to a ceremonial singer for his service at a ritual. The Navajos believed that good things did not come free and that such payments had to be made if a ceremony were to be successfully performed.

The Navajos' spiritual beliefs were not a religion in the conventional sense.

That term is in many ways too narrow to describe what the Navajos believed and practiced. Some understanding of the tribe's beliefs may be gained through consideration of a single Navajo word—*hozho*. Hozho is the combination of many ideas, including beauty, happiness, harmony, and goodness. It summarizes the basic goal and ultimate value of the Navajo world.

As recorded in the tribe's own stories of emergence, the Navajos knew that the world was fragile and that hozho was difficult to achieve and maintain. The world included a great many good things, but it also contained much evil. Some potentially evil things—such as snakes, bears, and lightning—had to be contained or controlled, because they were harmful if not dealt with properly.

The Navajos believed that all people, knowingly or otherwise, could fall under the contaminating influence of these elements. Many rituals of Navajo ceremonies were meant to help people overcome such influences and restore hozho. These rituals were performed to heal particular patients and were presided over by singers, whom non-Indians might view as both doctors and priests. The rites performed by singers are known as *chantways*.

Navajo ceremonies were extremely complex and therefore very difficult for novices to learn and memorize flawlessly. Some of the most elaborate ones took a full nine days to perform. A young man wishing to become a singer apprenticed himself to an experienced man who knew a particular ceremony or a few ceremonies. (Because of their great complexity, no one knew all the chantways.) The rituals had to be learned properly and then performed exactly right to achieve the desired effect. The Navajos believed that the chantways attracted the attention of the Holy People. If these supernatural beings judged that a chantway was being performed correctly, they would reciprocate by curing the patient.

Because a person's life could be disrupted in many ways, many ceremonies came to exist for restoring hozho. Navajos suffering from poor health, uneasiness, or bad luck would consult with a man or woman who had the power to diagnose their problem and prescribe an appropriate ritual to cure them. For example, a man could become unbalanced if he wandered into the pueblolike ruins of the villages of the Anasazis, a people who had vanished from the Southwest before the Navajos had migrated from the north. One ceremony that was commonly employed for this type of problem was the *nidah'*, known to non-Indians as the squaw dance. According to the Navajos' ancient stories, this ceremony originated when Monster Slayer, one of Changing Woman's two sons, fell ill. The Holy People and the Navajos themselves created the nidah' to heal him.

The nidah' was held over six days and involved a lead singer and his helpers, the patient, the patient's family members who sponsored the ritual, and other relatives and friends. Although

Three men dressed in the masks, collars, and head ornaments worn by participants in the Navajo ritual known as the Night Chant.

the nidah' was designed primarily to cure an ill person, it also brought people together because many people had to work cooperatively to make it possible. They had to pay ceremonial leaders, build temporary shelters for visitors, feed those in attendance, and gather gifts to offer the participants. Thus the nidah', like religious ceremonies the world over, was also a social function.

Some Navajo rituals were performed not to restore hozho but to promote it. These rituals presented people with good wishes and protected them from evil. One example of such a ritual was the Blessingway rite, a core observance of the Navajos' traditional beliefs. Variations of the Blessingway rite were performed for many different purposes, such as protecting sheep herds, blessing a new marriage, helping an expectant mother in childbirth, giving strength to an apprentice singer, or shielding a warrior from his enemies.

A Navajo man making a drypainting from pulverized sandstone and charcoal. This drypainting was used during a ceremony to help heal a sick child in 1954.

The Blessingway rite generally began at sundown and was performed without interruption over the course of two nights and one day. During the first night, participants recited prayers and songs while the beneficiary of the ceremony held a sacred bundle, called the mountain soil bundle, to his or her chest. This bundle, made of buckskin, contained smaller packets, each holding small scoops of earth from the tops of the four sacred mountains. More songs and prayers were said the follow-

ing day. The Blessingway rite concluded with the participants singing throughout the final night.

One version of the Blessingway rite was the kinaalda, the four-day ceremony performed for Navajo girls when they reached puberty and before they married. It not only blessed a young Navajo woman but also gave her the chance to learn from older women about their expectations for her as an adult. Traditionally, these expectations included being a good mother and wife, a skilled weaver, and a strong, patient, responsible person. During each day of the kinaalda, a girl would leave the hogan where the ceremony took place at dawn and run for a considerable distance, thus literally following in the footsteps of untold numbers of women before her. During the ceremony, which was arranged by each girl's mother, the young woman received much advice from older women about married life. The kinaalda was a happy occasion, and through it a young Navajo woman became an integral and important member of her people in both her own eyes and those of her family and community.

In some curative Navajo ceremonies, a drypainting (also called a sandpainting) was made by a helper under the supervision of the singer. These images were not actually formed with paint, but with dry pigments made from pulverized white, yellow, and red sandstone and crushed charcoal. The powders were shaped by the helper into patterns on the floor of the patient's hogan. Drypaintings ranged in size from less than 1 to more than 20 feet in diameter, took many hours to create, and were actively used in the final portion of the ceremony. The singer put his palms, moistened with herbal medicine, on top of the drypainting. After the painting's images were transferred to his hands, he placed his palms on the patient's body. This act linked the patient with the drypainting's sacred figures and thus assisted the healing process. At the end of the ceremony, the singer had what remained of the drypainting destroyed. After a drypainting was used in a ritual, the Navajos believed its reason for existence had come to an end.

In the years following the Navajos' migration to the Southwest, they lived in small communities spread over a wide territory. These communities were connected only loosely for political and military purposes. Sometimes a local leader would come to speak for several communities or lead a large group of people into battle against other Indian groups (especially the Utes to the north) or, later, against the Spanish. But although the various Navajo communities shared a single culture, they did not compose one political state or military unit. There was no one chief for all the people.

By the early 17th century, the Navajos had acquired horses, and their mobility increased. This permitted them to graze their sheep over a wider range and drive them into the shade of the mountains during the summer

An old Navajo man, photographed in 1914, holding a bow and arrow.

months. It also enabled them occasionally to raid other Indian people or the Spanish colonists in the region for food, horses, and other goods. These groups, in turn, sometimes raided Navajo communities.

Soon the Navajos pushed westward into lands claimed by the Spanish in what is now New Mexico and Arizona. The tribe generally avoided contact with the colonists, who were still largely concentrated in communities near Pueblo settlements along the Rio Grande. However, the Navajos did have some relations with Spanish

people. Navajo children were sometimes baptized in the Catholic church,
for example, and Navajo people taken
captive in military raids were sometimes sold into slavery. Despite this
contact with Christianity and European
culture, the Navajo people maintained
many of their traditional customs.

In 1680, many Pueblo Indians re-
belled against the religious, political,
and economic control of the colonizing
Spaniards. Led by a man named Popay
from San Juan Pueblo in present-day
northern New Mexico, the Pueblos attacked the Spanish settlements in their
territory and killed many of the inhabitants. The Pueblos then drove the survivors south. However, the Spanish
soon returned to the region seeking re-
venge. Some Pueblos then fled from
their homes and relocated on Navajo
lands. Despite language differences,
communication increased between the
Pueblos and the Navajos, as did the influences each group had on the other's
way of life.

Today it is often difficult to tell who
learned what from whom. It is known,
however, that some Navajo men married women from such communities as
Jemez Pueblo, and their descendants
incorporated elements of Pueblo culture into the daily lives of the Navajos.
Because many Pueblo people were
skilled farmers, the Navajos may have
learned ways to improve their agricultural methods from this association,
even though they themselves had been
farming for generations prior to the
1680 Pueblo revolt.

*A 1978 painting, by Paul St. James, of the
Pollen Boy, a Navajo symbol of fertility and
happiness. After corn became an important
crop to the tribe in the early 1700s, corn
pollen was often used in Navajo ceremonies.*

In the early 18th century, corn became a central element of Navajo culture, both as a food and as a symbol,
after it was introduced by the Pueblos.
Corn pollen came to be used in Navajo
ceremonies, often to represent fertility
or prosperity. The growth of the corn-
stalk was likened to the growth of the
Navajo people themselves. In the
tribe's stories, it associated the plant
with the Holy People. The planting of
corn thus was linked with the Navajos'
origin.

The tribe's adoption of other Indian
people, new crops, and European livestock during the 1600s and 1700s was
key to the development of modern Na-

vajo culture. The Navajos expanded and thrived because they took in elements of other cultures. Over the course of time, they even came to associate many of these relatively recent cultural acquisitions with their earliest days. They made them part of their legendary past. They made them Navajo.

During these same years, the descendants of the original Spanish colonists grew in number and became increasingly independent of their mother country. In the early 1800s, these people revolted against Spanish control and founded the modern nation of Mexico. At that time, Mexico extended into much of western North America, including what are now the states of Texas, New Mexico, Arizona, Colorado, Utah, Nevada, and California. But the vast majority of the Mexican population in the early 19th century resided south of this area. The non-Indian population of the Southwest remained sparse.

In the turmoil following its revolt against Spain, the new nation of Mexico was poorly equipped to defend the northernmost stretches of its borders. In early 1836, settlers in Texas revolted in turn against the Mexican government and established the Republic of Texas. At the request of the republic's citizens, the United States annexed Texas in 1845. However, Mexico refused to acknowledge the legality of the annexation. In the conflict that ensued—the Mexican War of 1846–48—the United States won a crushing victory. It promptly seized the entire Southwest, allowing American settlers to journey westward into this region.

By the mid-19th century, Americans had begun to arrive in Navajo country. Fortunately, the Navajos had established over hundreds of years a firm foundation for their own culture. But the Americans were soon to present an unparalleled challenge to the Navajo cultural world. ▲

Navajo leader Manuelito, photographed in 1874.

3

THE
LONG WALK

On February 2, 1848, the Mexican War came to an end when Mexico and the United States signed the Treaty of Guadalupe Hidalgo. Under its terms, the Mexican government ceded to the United States more than 1.2 million square miles of territory, including much of present-day New Mexico, Arizona, Colorado, Utah, Nevada, and California, in exchange for $15 million and other considerations. The two sides gave no thought, however, to the Indian people who had lived in the Southwest long before either nation had even existed.

The Treaty of Guadalupe Hidalgo brought rapid change to the Navajo world. American settlers swiftly began to travel westward to the new lands the United States had acquired. Just as quickly, the U.S. government moved to exert control over the Southwest. On August 31, 1849, U.S. representatives James Calhoun and Colonel John Washington, accompanied by some American soldiers, held a conference with a group of Navajo people in the Chuska Mountains of what is now northeastern Arizona. The American officials hoped to explain their government's plans for building forts and peacefully settling in the region.

Unfortunately, the meeting ended abruptly in an outburst of violence. The Navajos attempted to leave the conference after a dispute erupted over a horse that one visitor, a Mexican guide, claimed had been stolen from him. In the ensuing clash, soldiers shot and killed seven Navajos, including an influential leader named Narbona. The survivors told other Navajos about the incident, spreading fear and hatred of the hostile intruders among the tribespeople.

Among those most embittered by Narbona's death was his son-in-law Manuelito, who also was a significant Navajo leader. He and some other prominent Navajos, such as Barboncito, who was both a political and religious leader, grew angry about the Americans' presence on their land. Others, such as Zarcilla Largo and Ganado Mucho, were inclined to accommodate the newcomers and signed a series of treaties with the United States. However, because no one leader had the power to speak for all Navajos, most Navajos had little knowledge of these agreements.

In the early 1850s, the U.S. Army constructed a fort in the heart of Navajo country. Its name, Fort Defiance, suggests the antagonism the Navajos and the American soldiers felt for each other. Relations between the two groups were marked by increasing tension and unease. In July 1858, some Navajos expressed their hatred of the fort's commanding officer by killing his black slave, who was known as Jim. The commander, Captain William T. H. Brooks, demanded that the Navajos bring to him the individuals responsible for Jim's murder. Zarcilla Largo offered instead to give Brooks some money as compensation, but the commander refused to accept it. A group of Navajos then brought Brooks the body of a Mexican they had killed and identified him

as Jim's murderer. Brooks was not convinced and dispatched troops into the countryside. These forces eventually killed some Navajos who may have known nothing of the original dispute.

At the end of April 1860, Manuelito and Barboncito, determined to eliminate the American presence, led about a thousand warriors in a massive attack on Fort Defiance. The Navajos almost took the fort, but the U.S. troops finally drove the warriors back.

Despite the army's victory, skirmishes continued to occur. One of the most tragic took place on September 22, 1861, at Fort Fauntleroy in modern-day New Mexico. In accordance with the terms of a treaty negotiated between the United States and the tribe earlier that year, a group of Navajos traveled to the fort to receive rations of food. As was common on ration days, a series of horse races were held, on which both the Navajos and the U.S. soldiers bet heavily. The Navajos accused the Americans of cheating, but the race judges (all of whom were soldiers) ruled that the charges were unfounded. A dispute followed, and in the confusion the fort's commander, Colonel Manuel Chaves, ordered troops to open fire on the Indians. Twelve women and children were among the Navajos killed.

By the early 1860s, U.S. Army officials were convinced that a major military campaign had to be waged to compel the Navajos to submit to federal authority. This perspective was quickly adopted by Brigadier General James

Carleton, who was named commander of the U.S. Army in New Mexico Territory in the fall of 1862.

General Carleton had a problem. The Civil War had broken out a year earlier, but the battles between the Union (the North) and the Confederacy (the South) were being fought almost exclusively east of the Mississippi River. Many U.S. troops stationed in New Mexico Territory were posted to the east for combat duty. As a result, New Mexican settlers were inadequately defended from Indian raids on their livestock. The soldiers who remained also grew increasingly edgy because of their isolation from the Civil War battlefront.

Carleton wanted to let his soldiers exercise their thirst for battle on enemies closer to home—the Navajos and the nearby Mescalero Apaches. The general's idea of fighting these tribes was quickly approved by the governor of New Mexico Territory. It was also supported by the territory's non-Indian population, which felt vulnerable to Indian attacks.

General Carleton was actually interested in more than simply subduing the Indians. He thought Apache and Navajo country might conceal a wealth of untapped gold ore and other minerals. In order to open the region to full-scale exploration by miners, Carleton hoped to round up the scattered Indian peoples in the region and relocate them to the newly established Fort Sumner on the Pecos River in what is now east-

A watercolor of Narbona, based on a sketch by Richard H. Kern. The Navajo leader sat for his portrait on August 31, 1849, the day he was killed at the hands of U.S. soldiers.

central New Mexico. Confined in a nearby area called the Bosque Redondo (Spanish for "round grove"), they could be overseen easily, and by fewer troops than were needed to police the Indians' traditional territory. Carleton also looked upon the establishment of this reservation—the tract of land to which the Indians would be officially restricted—as a means to change the Navajos' and Apaches' traditional ways of life. On the reservation they would be a captive audience for whites seeking

Colonel Kit Carson (left), leader of the U.S. troops who defeated the Navajos in 1863, and Brigadier General James Carleton, architect of the plan to relocate those who surrendered to Bosque Redondo, in eastern New Mexico.

a colonel in the New Mexico territorial militia. Carson agreed to help Carleton, but not without serious and persistent doubts as to the wisdom of the plan. Nonetheless, Carson and his troops began to battle the Mescalero Apaches. Within six months the army had defeated the tribe and relocated the Mescalero Apache population to Fort Sumner.

In July 1863, Carson and his men journeyed to Fort Defiance to begin their campaign to subdue the Navajo people. According to Carleton's explicit instructions, all Indians who refused to surrender and relocate ran the risk of being killed. But his message was never communicated to the Navajos. As Carson's men moved into their country, the Navajos fled. They were far more numerous than the Mescalero Apaches, and the rugged terrain increased the challenge of tracking the Indians down. The colonel found himself compelled to take drastic measures to comply with Carleton's ruthless orders.

Stories passed down through generations teach the Navajos of today about this very difficult period in tribal history. The soldiers marched through Canyon de Chelly, in the heart of their country, spoiling wells and burning cornfields and peach orchards. Sometimes they shot Navajos and their livestock without provocation or even any warning.

The winter of 1863–64 was especially severe. Many Navajos went hungry because the army's intrusion made it impossible for them to farm and store

to "civilize" them by preaching Christianity and teaching them other non-Indian values. Held long enough, Carleton reasoned, the Indians might be compelled to assimilate into mainstream American society.

To spearhead the initial stages of his program, Carleton selected Kit Carson. A legendary trapper and explorer, Carson had been living in Taos and working as the government's agent, or representative, among the Ute people. He had resigned this post, however, after the Civil War broke out, to become food. Some people began to surrender in groups so that they might remain together. These groups gathered at Fort Wingate and nearby Fort Defiance in central New Mexico Territory, the points from which they were to begin their journey to Bosque Redondo. It soon became apparent that there were far more Navajo people than Carleton had anticipated. By the end of 1864, some 8,000 Navajos had surrendered. All would be forced to endure the indignity of the march to Fort Sumner and confinement along the Pecos River.

Tales abound of the suffering and ill-treatment incurred by the Navajos during the Long Walk, as the 250-mile march to Bosque Redondo is known today. Navajos who put up any resistance during the Long Walk were physically abused or even shot. Women who gave birth along the way were allowed no time to rest. Old people and children were sorely pressed to keep up with their families.

Some Navajos escaped the hardship of the Long Walk. Perhaps as many as several thousand fled north and west, into the isolated canyons of what is now northern Arizona or onto the Black Mesa, a high, remote plateau within sight of Canyon de Chelly. The great

Canyon de Chelly, in the heart of Navajo country. Kit Carson's soldiers stormed through the canyon and subjugated its inhabitants in the fall of 1863.

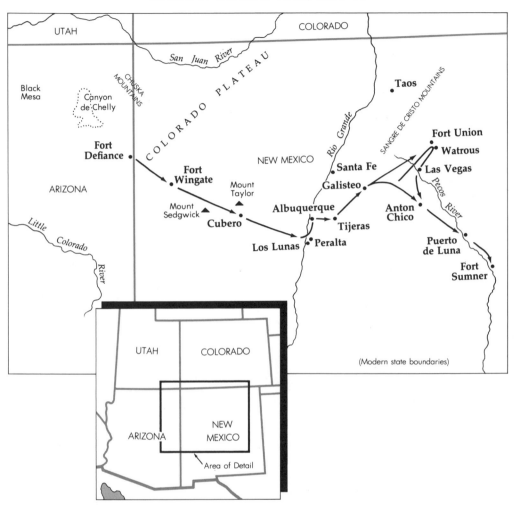

Navajo leaders Manuelito and Barboncito also resisted relocation for some time. Manuelito finally surrendered and arrived at Fort Sumner in 1866. His capitulation prompted Barboncito, Ganado Mucho, and others to turn themselves over to the American authorities.

At Fort Sumner, the Navajos suffered greatly from their confinement and their separation from their homeland. The government had negotiated contracts with non-Indians to provide food rations for the Navajos. However, most of these suppliers were corrupt and made huge profits by giving the

Indians meager rations of spoiled food. Many Navajos grew ill with digestive problems. Some also complained that the region's salty water gave them dysentery. The poor soil along the Pecos River produced scanty harvests, which were ravaged by cutworms. And although the army had agreed to protect the Navajos at Fort Sumner, Comanches and other tribes raided the outpost.

Evidence mounted that Carleton's experiment had failed. The general increasingly came under criticism, not only from Indians but also from neighboring non-Indians who thought his program was unjust, ill conceived, and poorly managed. Some simply wanted the Navajos removed from the vicinity, believing they could live elsewhere at less expense to the government. Eventually Carleton could no longer fend off his critics, and he was relieved of his command in September 1866. In January 1867, the Bureau of Indian Affairs (BIA), the federal agency in the Department of the Interior that had been founded in 1824 to manage governmental relations with Indians, took over responsibility for the Navajos' welfare from the U.S. Army.

During the years following the Civil War, the U.S. government reassessed its policy toward all Indians. Officials were especially concerned about dealing with Indians in the West. The number of Americans settling in the region was rising and was expected to increase even more as America's first transcontinental railroad neared completion. To accommodate these settlers, federal policymakers hoped to sign treaties with Indian peoples that would include terms for their confinement on well-defined reservations. To this end, Congress formed the U.S. Indian Peace Commission, a delegation composed of military men and civilians that headed west to negotiate treaties with various tribes. Two of its members, Colonel Samuel F. Tappan and General William Tecumseh Sherman, visited the Navajos at Fort Sumner in the spring of 1868.

At the commisioner's request, the tribe chose 10 men—with Barboncito as principal spokesman—to represent the Navajos in these discussions. These representatives argued and pleaded with Tappan and Sherman to allow them to return to their homeland. At a meeting on May 28, Barboncito told the visitors:

> The bringing of us here has caused a great decrease of our numbers, many of us have died, also a great number of our animals. . . . Our Grandfathers had no idea of living in any other country except our own. . . . When the Navajos were first created four mountains and four rivers were pointed out to us, inside of which we should live; that [which] was to be our country was given to us by the first woman of the Navajos' tribe.

In response, Sherman spoke of the federal policy of relocating, or removing, tribes to Indian Territory, an area

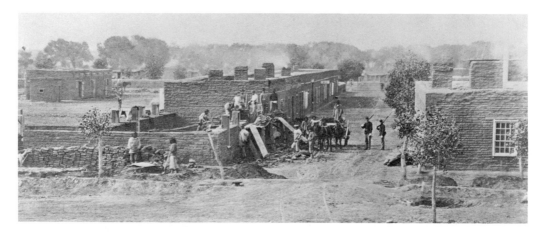

A photograph from the 1860s of Navajo laborers building quarters for U.S. troops at Fort Sumner while armed soldiers oversee their work.

in what is now Oklahoma where many eastern Indians had been given reservations. Because the Navajos were unhappy in their present home, he asked whether they would come to live in Indian Territory instead. Sherman explained that if they did not want to pursue that option, he would be willing to consider allowing them to return to their homeland. But, he added, if they did go back, they would have to live peacefully within clearly defined boundaries.

Barboncito replied, "I hope to God you will not ask me to go to any other country than my own." The next day at talks to negotiate the Navajos' return home, he said:

> After we get back to our country it will brighten up again and the Navajos will be as happy as the land, black clouds will rise and there will be plenty of rain. Corn will grow in

abundance and everything will look happy.

On June 1, 1868, following two more days of meetings, the Navajo representatives signed a treaty with the U.S. government. The document was ratified in the following month by the U.S. Senate. The treaty established the initial boundaries of the Navajo reservation, which included only about one-fourth of the tribe's traditional territory. The reservation was a rectangular parcel comprising 3.5 million acres in what is now northeastern Arizona and northwestern New Mexico. One article of the treaty required that the United States provide a teacher for every 30 Navajo children between the ages 6 and 18 "who can be induced or compelled to attend school." The government also pledged to give the Navajo people seeds and farming equipment and to purchase 15,000 sheep and goats and

500 beef cattle for their use. In turn, the Navajos agreed not to oppose the construction of any railroad or roads through the reservation, not to raid non-Indian settlements, and not to block the building of any military posts in their midst.

With the Navajos' return to their ancestral homeland, the people's future suddenly seemed bright once more. Unlike many other tribes, the Navajos had managed to hold on to a significant section of their territory rather than being forced to endure permanent removal to alien ground. Living again within the boundaries of the four sacred mountains gave the Navajos cultural continuity. They knew the land and what it could provide for them in the years to come. If they had been compelled to remain outside of their true home, the history of the Navajos might have been very different. But now, as Barboncito had said, they looked forward to being as happy as the land itself. ▲

Barboncito, one of the Navajo leaders who negotiated the 1868 treaty with the United States that permitted the Navajos to return to their homeland.

A delegation of Navajo representatives who traveled to Washington, D.C., in 1874 to discuss the provisions of the 1868 treaty with President Ulysses S. Grant.

THE
WEAVING TOGETHER
OF A
PEOPLE

Glad as the Navajos were to leave Fort Sumner in 1868, they faced significant problems upon their return to their homeland. The Long Walk and the years at Bosque Redondo had sapped the strength of many people and disrupted many families. The tribe was allowed to return to only a portion of the land it had occupied in years past. Despite the government's assurance that the army would protect the Navajos, other Indian peoples continued to raid their lands. Hunger also became a problem when, after a season of bad weather, many of the first crops the Navajos had planted on their reservation yielded small harvests.

But in many ways the old days were gone, and a new era had begun. Despite their hardships, the people felt fortunate to be living within the four sacred mountains once again. They were also encouraged by the government's adherence to the terms of the 1868 treaty. In accordance with the agreement, the U.S. government sent a teacher, Charity Gaston, to Fort Defiance to teach a few Navajo children. The government also gave the Navajos the livestock promised in the treaty. The people slowly began to spread across the reservation, feeling more confident about their future.

Ironically, the government's failed relocation of the Navajos to Bosque Redondo ultimately had some positive results. During this tribulation, the government had treated the Navajos as one people. This changed the Navajos' perception of themselves. Living in independent communities scattered over a vast area, the Navajos had previously had little sense of tribal unity. But now, having experienced the horrors of the Long Walk, they began to perceive the need to work together to survive and prosper. Thus the foundation of what would eventually be the Navajo Nation was laid in the 1860s.

As their population grew and their sheep multiplied, the Navajos began to find the 3.5-million acre reservation inadequate. In the late 19th century, while most Indian tribes were losing land, the Navajos, through their government-appointed Indian agents, began to demand more territory from the government. Most of the land they sought had been used by them before the Long Walk.

Living in a region then largely neglected by settlers, the Navajos were able to persuade the government to make, by executive order, three additions to their reservation during the final decades of the 1800s. The first, granted on October 29, 1878, added a narrow rectangular strip of some 960,000 acres next to the western border of their original reservation. On January 6, 1880, a U-shaped area of nearly 100,000 acres to the south was annexed. Finally, in 1884, more than 2 million acres along what is now the Arizona-Utah borderline were added. This beautiful country had been a place of refuge for many Navajos who had escaped the Long Walk.

In 1882, the federal government, again by executive order, also established a reservation for the Hopi Indians. The Hopis, like the Pueblo and Zuni peoples, were descendants of the prehistoric Anasazi Indians and had lived in the Southwest for hundreds of years. The Hopis' homes were concentrated on and around three mesas (flat-topped mountains), within their new reservation. The Hopi reservation boundaries were drawn to include lands the Navajos were already using, and the executive order stipulated that the Hopi land could be occupied by "other Indians as the Secretary of the Interior may see fit to settle thereon." Consequently, the Hopis and Navajos began to share portions of the Hopi reservation. But this uneasy arrangement did not entirely please either tribe and would result in great problems between the Navajos and the Hopis decades later.

During the late 1800s, the size of the Navajos' herds of livestock increased dramatically. In 1891, U.S. special agent Dana K. Shipley conducted a survey and concluded that the Navajo people then numbered roughly 17,000. Shipley also concluded that they owned nearly 19,000 horses, 9,000 cattle, 500 mules, and more than 1.5 million sheep. These figures, though probably inflated, clearly indicate the huge growth of the herds. A more reliable source estimates conservatively that the number of sheep and goats soared from perhaps 40,000 in 1868 to nearly 800,000 at the end of the 19th century.

Such staggering increases, combined with an expanding land base,

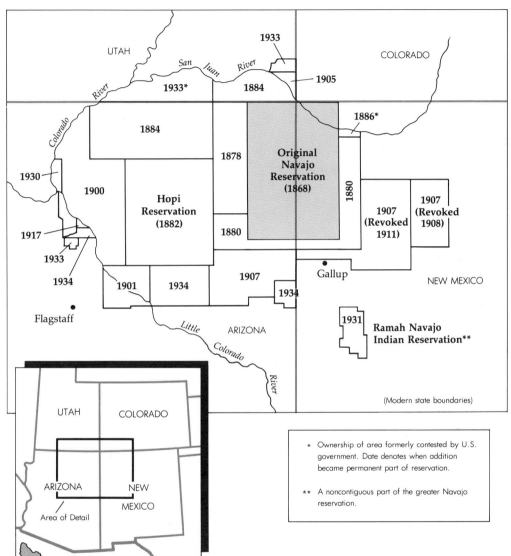

suggest that the Navajo were prospering. The tribe was without a doubt staging an impressive comeback from the Bosque Redondo era. However, there was a price to be paid for this headlong development. The mountainous lands of the harsh, dry Southwest had never supported lush greenery. By the late 1800s, the skyrocketing Navajo livestock population had begun to deplete the area's already sparse vegetation. Sheep often eat grass down to its roots.

Cattle and horses, with their great weight and sharp hooves, sometimes trample more grass than they consume. Once vegetation has been ravaged by overgrazing, the exposed land often erodes, as strong winds and flash floods carry away the loose, mineral-rich topsoil, leaving behind only sterile, barren gulleys.

The problem of soil erosion loomed even before the turn of the century. By 1883, Indian agent Dennis Riordan reported to the BIA in Washington that the Navajos had "too many sheep" and "an enormous number of useless ponies." He believed that their total sheep herd should be cut by half or more to prevent overgrazing and avert the destruction of their land. Riordan also said that the Navajos had to change their thinking about horses. They did not need so many, he said, but merely liked having great numbers of them. In his opinion, the problem of soil erosion would not be solved until the Navajos changed their attitude about these animals.

The Navajos, however, believed that the solution lay not in reducing their livestock herds but in further increasing their amount of grazing land. Federal policy seemed to encourage this perspective. In the first decade of the 20th century, four more additions were made to the reservation by executive order. The government was willing to give this land to the Navajos because northern Arizona's relatively small

An early-20th-century photograph of Navajo lands drastically ravaged by soil erosion.

non-Indian population had little interest in settling this forbidding region.

As the Navajos prospered during the late 19th and early 20th centuries, a significant institution began to dot their countryside—the trading post. Usually established and owned by non-Indians, trading posts on the reservation were often the only places of business for many miles around. Naturally, each became a center for local social life. People gathered not only to trade but to visit with one another.

As its name implies, the transactions at a trading post usually involved barter rather than money. The Navajos quickly learned to be shrewd bargainers, offering the traders crops, raw wool, or other agrarian products in exchange for goods such as metal pots, fabric, coffee, and flour. Traders sometimes extended credit if the Indian could provide the trader with a pawn— an item left as security. The pawn could be recovered later, when the Navajo had products to pay back the extended credit. If the item was left beyond a specific length of time, however, the trader was entitled to sell it for whatever money it might bring. The Navajos commonly used their jewelry or their intricately woven blankets as pawns. Traders quickly recognized that there was a market among non-Indian customers for these beautiful objects. Soon the traders prized blankets and jewelry not as pawns but as trade items that were as valuable as livestock and agricultural products. In this fashion, traders soon came to have a strong personal interest in the expansion and diversity of the Navajo economy.

Traders such as Lorenzo Hubbell of Ganado, J. B. Moore of Crystal, and Thomas Keam of Keams Canyon encouraged Navajo women to weave larger blankets that could be used as rugs. The traders then sent out colorful catalogs to merchants in the East that advertised the exceptional creativity of the weavers. With the coming of railroads, such as the Santa Fe line, commerce between the eastern and western United States increased, and there was soon a growing market for Navajo craftwork. Because most Navajos did not speak English and rarely left the reservation, traders became influential intermediaries between the tribe and non-Indian customers.

Exercising this influence, traders suggested designs they believed would appeal to their customers and discouraged imitations of non-Indian rug patterns. Using vertical looms they had adopted from the Pueblos, Navajo women living in different regions gradually developed distinctive local styles. They also began to use newly available commercial dyes as well as traditional vegetable pigments to color their wool. But even though the weavers saved considerable time by using commercial dyes, each rug often took hundreds of hours to make.

Traders also encouraged Navajo men to become master silversmiths. Some Navajos had learned silversmithing from Mexicans during the decades before the Long Walk. In the late 19th

The interior of a trading post in the Red Rock community in 1932. In the late 19th and early 20th centuries, non-Indian-owned trading posts were established throughout the Navajo reservation.

century, trader Lorenzo Hubbell brought Mexican silversmiths to the reservation to teach more Navajo men this skill, and soon these students instructed still more tribesmen. Using Mexican and U.S. coins (such as silver dollars) as raw material, these smiths fashioned intricate belt buckles, buttons, bracelets, rings, earrings, necklaces, horse bridles, and other items.

By the 1890s, Navajo silversmiths had begun setting turquoise into their jewelry. This bluish mineral was mined nearby and brought to the reservation by traders. The juxtaposition of turquoise and silver rapidly became a distinctively Navajo look. This jewelry was soon as popular within the tribe as it was with non-Indians.

Traders, though influential, were not the sole non-Indian force within the

Navajo world at this time. Christian missionaries began to arrive on the reservation in hopes of converting the Indians to their faith. Among the earliest missionaries to come to Navajo country were the Presbyterians, who arrived about 1869 and built a mission in Ganado near Hubbell's trading post. In 1906 they added to this the Ganado Mission School.

Given the proximity of large Mormon settlements in Utah, it is not surprising that the Mormon church was also a presence on the reservation. As early as the 1870s, some Navajos were baptized by Mormon missionaries. A small Mormon settlement also existed in Moenkopi (near modern-day Tuba City, Arizona), although church members later moved away as the reservation expanded.

The Prebysterians and Mormons were followed in the 1890s by priests of the Franciscan order of the Catholic church. They located their mission, St. Michaels, near Fort Defiance, about 25 miles east of Ganado. The Franciscans subsequently founded St. Michaels Mission School there in 1902. While attempting to convert the Navajos, the priests became interested in their culture. St. Michaels soon emerged as a center for the study of the Navajo language, religion, and way of life.

The Presbyterians and Catholics were soon joined by members of the Methodist and Christian Reformed churches. Both denominations also constructed schools. The Christian Reformed church established a mission,

Rehoboth, in 1898 and built the Rehoboth Mission School in 1903 near the town of Gallup. The Navajo Methodist Mission School, originally situated near Shiprock, was moved to Farmington, New Mexico, east of the reservation, in 1912.

Federal policy during this period encouraged churches to become major participants in Indian education. Mission schools educated many Navajo children who would grow up to become tribal leaders. Although such schools had widely varying views of, and approaches to, Navajo culture, parents who selected them generally did so because of their significant differences from BIA schools. Often the priests at mission schools had put in years of service to the Navajo community, whereas teacher turnover in BIA schools was rapid. Mission schools also were usually (though not invariably) more responsive than BIA schools to parental opinions.

In contrast, the territorial governments of Arizona and New Mexico showed little interest in educating Navajos. However, the federal government continued to fund the Navajo school it had established in the 1860s at Fort Defiance. The BIA founded a few others as well, including one in 1887 at Keams Canyon (attended by both Navajo and Hopi pupils) and another in 1895 at Tohatchi. A small number of Navajo students attended off-reservation federal boarding schools, such as those founded at Albuquerque in 1886, at Santa Fe in 1890, and at Phoenix in 1891. A few (usually older) students went to the leading federal Indian schools of the day—Haskell Institute in Lawrence, Kansas, and Carlisle Indian Industrial School in Carlisle, Pennsylvania.

Most public education of Indians at this time aimed to assimilate students into mainstream American society. Teachers taught in English and generally discouraged or even prohibited use of the Navajo language. Courses emphasized non-Indian values, priorities, and needs.

It is scarcely surprising that many Navajo parents, especially those who followed tribal traditions closely, opposed an educational program that tried to make their children part of an alien society. Moreover, they often needed their children to assist with herding the sheep and other necessary work at home. Therefore, most Navajo children either did not attend school or went for only a short time. Sometimes parents chose one child in their family to attend school while his or her siblings worked. Many non-Indian parents across the United States did likewise during this era, when even a high school education was out of reach for most children.

Many angry confrontations occurred when agents or school truant officers attempted to compel Navajo children to attend school. Parents often barred the doorway of their hogan and refused to let these officials take their children. On one occasion in 1893, Dana K. Shipley tried to seize children against their will and force them to attend the Fort Defiance boarding school many miles away. A Navajo leader named Black Horse then apprehended Shipley. The agent barely escaped serious injury from furious parents.

However the Navajos may have felt about the world outside the reservation, that world encroached increasingly upon their own. In the early 1900s, geological surveys revealed the possible presence of oil on Navajo land. In 1921, after a major oil discovery was made in northwestern New Mexico, the Midwest Refining Company gained permission from the BIA to negotiate with the Navajos for the right to drill on the reservation. Company officials were eager to begin talks but were hindered by one problem: They had no idea with whom they were to negotiate. The Navajo reservation was a very large area with a substantial population. The Navajos had only recently begun to think of themselves as one people, and the old spirit of local independence had not entirely disappeared. Who dared speak for all the Navajos?

By the 1920s, the BIA had divided the Navajo reservation into six administrative areas. These were called the Southern, Western, San Juan (Northern), Pueblo Bonito (Eastern), Leupp, and Moqui jurisdictions. (The Moqui Jurisdiction would later become the Hopi Indian Agency.) The BIA assigned one agent to each division. When an important problem arose, an agent might call together certain Navajos in his division for a special meeting. The

Navajo people had no interdivision council, however.

Potential oil income created a number of questions that the Navajos needed a central governing body to solve. For example, the Midwest Refining Company planned to drill near Shiprock, so the people living there would be more inconvenienced by the venture. Yet the oil money might, theoretically, be used to benefit Navajos in all areas. Somehow the tribe had to determine who should reap the rewards of the business deal when the drawbacks would be felt by only one portion of the population.

Initially, the Navajos of the Shiprock area met in informal councils to consider possible leases. But they did not act quickly enough to satisfy either the BIA or the Midwest Refining Company. In 1922, the BIA selected prominent Navajo leaders Chee Dodge, Charlie Mitchell, and Dugal Chee Bekis to serve as a business council for the whole reservation. Dodge, the son of a Navajo mother and a Mexican father, was especially respected as an educated businessman, community leader, orator, and interpreter. All three leaders served their people thoughtfully. But they were not elected representatives, and the arrangement was clearly unsatisfactory in the long run.

The following year, a tribal council was established according to rules set forth by the BIA. The council was to be composed of 12 delegates and 12 alternates elected by the Navajo people. The size of the population of each division

A Navajo smith, photographed in 1915, making jewelry from silver coins.

would determine how many representatives it could send to the council. The area around Shiprock (the San Juan Jurisdiction) could have three delegates, and that around Fort Defiance (the Southern Jurisdiction) four, because these divisions included the largest number of people. The people of each division on the reservation then met and elected 12 councilmen whose names reflected the diversity of the Navajo population: George Bancroft, Todachene Bardony, Becenti Bega, Hosteen Begoiden Bega, Deshna Cahcheschillige, Hosteen Yazzie Jesus, Robert Martin, Jacob Morgan, Hosteen Nez, Hosteen Usahelin, Louis Watchman, and Zagenitzo. Even though the organization had been imposed upon the Navajos, who had mixed feelings about its very existence, the formation of the council was undeniably a significant step in the tribe's political unification.

The new Navajo Tribal Council held its first meeting on July 7, 1923, in Toadlena, New Mexico, and elected Chee Dodge as its chairman. The councilmen would not have long to wait before confronting some difficult questions. ▲

The first five chairmen of the Navajo Tribal Council, photographed in 1938 (left to right): Marcus Kanuho, Deshna Clah Cheschillige, Chee Dodge (founding chairman), Tom Dodge, and Henry Taliman.

THE TIME
OF
LIVESTOCK REDUCTION

The 1920s were the start of a period of intense political, social, and economic transition for the Navajo people. Although the political changes were most obvious and immediate, the social, and economic changes that began at this time would have an equally important effect on the tribe's immediate future.

During the 1920s, the newly formed Navajo Tribal Council annually held only one regular session, lasting but a few days. The council's primary business was to decide whether to lease land to oil companies that wanted to drill on the reservation. The council members studied each proposed lease carefully. As they became more experienced in these negotiations, they increasingly demanded that their people receive a fair royalty, or percentage of the oil companies' profits.

After several leases were approved, oilmen began to drill exploratory wells, a number of which proved to be dry holes—sites that yielded no oil. The small amount of oil obtained from the few producing wells was a disappointment to the oilmen and the Navajos alike. The royalty money that trickled into the tribal treasury was also less than overwhelming. The companies soon discovered oil in other regions of the Southwest, and by the end of the decade, most oilmen had turned their attention away from the Navajo reservation.

Although unsuccessful, the search for oil on the reservation had had the positive effect of forcing the creation of the council, which continued to be responsible for the tribe's well-being. And the council members took their job seriously. Rather than deciding to divide the relatively small oil revenue among the Navajos, giving each person a small sum of money, the council put the entire amount into a general tribal fund to benefit the Navajos as a whole. The sum was initially used as an emergency relief fund to help those stricken by natural disasters such as severe droughts. The council's decision to use the oil money to help the tribe as a group was in keeping with traditional Navajo values. It would also serve as an important precedent later, when the council would have to deal with much larger sums.

Although the council was effective at solving problems that involved the entire tribe, it was not equipped to make decisions regarding all the many day-to-day local concerns of the Navajos. Another type of political organization was needed to deal appropriately with neighborhood problems. In 1927, John Hunter, the agent of one of the reservation's six divisions, devised such organizations within his jurisdiction. Hunter organized communities into *chapters*. The people in each chapter elected officers, who held meetings to discuss local issues.

The other divisions of the Navajo reservation quickly adopted the chapter system. It worked because it dealt with matters best handled locally. For example, two families might disagree over who had the right to graze sheep on a certain piece of land and ask their chapter leaders to settle the dispute. The Navajo people had for generations resolved this type of disagreement by discussing it with local leaders. The new procedure therefore simply formalized an existing tradition. An extra benefit was that the tribal council could meet with chapter representatives to learn about local issues and thereby keep in touch with common concerns. Eventually, nearly 100 chapters existed across the reservation. They were formed around the widely scattered Navajo communities and varied in size, but each usually comprised at least a few hundred people.

Despite the chapter system's success, chapter councils did not officially become part of the tribal government for many years. The same is true of two other branches of the Navajo government: its police force and court system. A Navajo court system had been authorized by the federal government in 1883 but was not instituted until 1891. Informal police forces had formed on occasion for specific tasks, such as retrieving stolen cattle, but a permanent corps of police developed only in the 1880s.

Such gradual and informal changes in Navajo society were, however, soon to be rushed under federal pressure, primarily because of the soil erosion issue. In 1928, Assistant Commissioner of Indian Affairs E. B. Meritt journeyed from Washington, D.C., to Leupp, Arizona, to tell Navajo councilmen that the federal government wanted the people eventually to limit the number of their sheep, horses, goats, and cattle. Two years later a BIA forester, William Zeh, completed a survey of Navajo lands and arrived at discouraging conclusions. Zeh called the Navajo range "deteriorating" and noted that one of the main reasons for this situation was the region's inadequate water supply. Herds had to travel long distances to get water, and the large numbers of livestock overgrazed the sparse vegetation during their journey. As a result, the region suffered further soil erosion.

In February 1931, BIA officials yet again met among themselves to discuss the growing problem. They concluded that Navajo herds would have to be reduced in number if the reservation land were ever to improve. The officials assumed that if the Navajo people could be made to understand the gravity of their predicament, they would willingly adopt stern measures.

The Navajos, however, saw their situation differently. Traders had long encouraged them to expand their

A chapter meeting at Shiprock in 1957. The chapter system, inaugurated in the 1930s, formalized the Navajos' tradition of allowing local leaders to settle disputes among people within a community.

flocks, and the federal government had over the years added a good deal of land to the reservation. The Navajos believed that if the government would only continue to increase their territory, these additions—along with more rain—would solve the problem perceived by the white men. A prolonged period of drought had in fact added to the soil erosion problem, but there was an element of wishful thinking in the Navajos' expectations of greater rainfall.

A view of Boulder Dam (now Hoover Dam) from Lookout Point in Nevada. Federal officials' concern over the erosion of Navajo land grew as silt from the reservation threatened the dam's workability.

A changing political situation outside the reservation also made enlarging the reservation difficult. The growing non-Indian population of Arizona and New Mexico, which had become states in 1912, had elected congressmen and senators who clamored against making public property part of Navajo country. They instead wanted public lands and money devoted to such projects as Boulder Dam, then under construction on the Colorado River in northwestern Arizona. The dam, later renamed Hoover Dam after President Herbert Hoover, would become on its completion in 1936 one of the largest in the world, providing flood control, irrigation, and electric power to the entire southwestern United States.

In the fall of 1932, following the onset of a severe economic depression throughout the United States, Franklin D. Roosevelt succeeded Hoover as president. Roosevelt appointed John Collier as his new commissioner of Indian affairs. Collier had become fascinated with Indian life while traveling through the Southwest. He became an impartial advocate of Indian rights during the 1920s, when he joined the Navajos' neighbors, the Pueblos, in their fight against a congressional bill that sought to diminish their territory. He had come to admire the Pueblos' traditional emphasis on community and, as commissioner of Indian affairs, wanted to help Indian people across the country achieve a brighter future. The programs he introduced at the BIA recognized the diversity of Indian cultures and supported Indians' right to be consulted in shaping federal Indian policy.

When Collier heard of the soil erosion in Navajo country and the tribe's need for more land, he became determined to use his position to help them. But he knew little about the Navajos' history and society, especially about the importance of livestock in their culture. Because of his lack of understanding of their way of life, Collier soon antagonized the Navajos, who came to regard this well-intentioned man as an enemy.

Collier believed that to save their ranges the Navajos should be granted more land and, at the same time, cut back on their livestock. He told tribal council members that if they would agree to livestock reduction he would be able to get them additional territory, along with local schools, water development, and federal jobs that were part of Roosevelt's New Deal program to revive the national economy. Collier was able to obtain congressional approval for two very small additions to the reservation on its northern and western boundaries and a larger extension on its southern border. But strong opposition by congressmen from New Mexico blocked any chance of expansion to the east. Although the actions of Congress were clearly beyond Collier's control, the Navajos felt he had failed to meet his part of the bargain when their reservation was not significantly enlarged.

Collier, however, felt he was doing his best and, moreover, doing the right

U.S. commissioner of Indian affairs John Collier in 1938. His program to forcibly reduce the Navajos' livestock herds made the tribe see him as one of its greatest enemies.

thing by compelling the Navajos to reduce their livestock. Factors other than land conservation influenced the commissioner's actions. The workability of Boulder Dam appeared endangered by the vast amount of silt that continued to erode from Navajo lands and run off into the Colorado River. Also, with the national economy so depressed, there was little if any demand on the free market for Navajo livestock. If the tribe was to make it through these difficult times, Collier concluded, he had no choice but to override the Navajos' objections to his course of action.

From about 1933 to 1935, livestock reduction was largely voluntary. Collier used funds from the Federal Emergency Relief Administration to purchase Navajo sheep and goats, which were then shipped off to be used to feed impoverished people elsewhere in the country. In an effort to cooperate, the Navajo Tribal Council voted that everyone in the tribe should accept a flat 10 percent reduction in their herds. But this cut proved to be only the first step in a drastic program that would last for more than a decade and affect the Navajos' entire way of life.

Even today the Navajos remember the years of livestock reduction with bitterness. The memories are fresh and strong because the people have passed the stories down from one generation to the next. The stories tell of sheep being forcibly taken from their owners, driven over the next hill or into the next valley, and then shot and left to rot. Beloved horses were also taken away and shot. Some Navajos went to jail for refusing to round up livestock or for fighting the agents who carried out the reduction program.

The Navajos were always paid at least a small amount for the livestock seized from them. But they resented the loss of their livestock—especially of their sheep—because they saw it as an attack not only upon their means of support but upon their very culture. Sheep were the traditional payment given to a singer for presiding over a sacred ceremony. The animals were also needed to feed visiting relatives and neighbors. Perhaps most important, Navajo children learned traditional tribal values and responsibilities by helping to care for their family's sheep herd. Without sheep, how could a child learn what it was to be a member of the people?

Not only the act of livestock reduction but the way in which it was done embittered the Navajos. After 1936, the government seemed to approach the program as a crusade to be carried out with a vengeance. Agents started forcibly taking away livestock without any explanation to the animals' owners. The government did dispatch employees to the reservation to help the Navajos and to try to persuade them to cooperate. But the agents performed their task too quickly and with too little sensitivity. The Navajo people could not see why they should surrender their precious sheep herds, built up over generations, to this man they had never met, this John Collier.

A resistance movement soon arose under the leadership of Jacob Morgan, a spokesman for the Navajos in the northern area of the reservation, near Shiprock. The people from this portion of the reservation expressed their anger at John Collier by voting overwhelmingly against reorganizing their tribal government according to the provisions of the Indian Reorganization Act (IRA) of 1934. This ground-breaking legislation radically changed federal Indian policy and had been strongly supported by Collier. Among the IRA's aims were the end of unregulated sale of Indian

continued on page 73

FROM SILVER AND WOOL

The Navajos have traditionally produced some of the best workers in silver and wool anywhere. Navajo silversmiths, usually men, can shape inert silver so that it flows like liquid and shimmers with the brilliance of the desert sun. Navajo weavers, traditionally women, work on simple wooden looms to create brilliantly colored blankets and rugs. The geometric patterns they use seem to echo the sharp lines of mesa, cliff, and canyon that characterize Navajo country.

Navajo women probably learned weaving from their Pueblo Indian neighbors in the late 1600s. Navajo men learned how to work silver from Mexican smiths in the early 1850s. But in neither case did the Navajo artisans simply imitate. Rather, they changed each craft to reflect their own taste and traditions and pushed them in artistic directions never imagined by their teachers.

In the 1870s, these two Navajo crafts came under powerful outside influences. Railroads reached the Southwest and trading posts multiplied, putting the tribe in touch with whites eager to pay for their crafts. Many Navajo artisans began altering their work to make it more appealing to white customers. For instance, they started to adorn their silver jewelry with turquoise and weave their first rugs, which whites preferred to blankets. Economic reality compelled the Navajos to make these changes. But in keeping with their old pattern, they did so on their own terms, creating new forms and styles that meshed with and enriched the Navajo way.

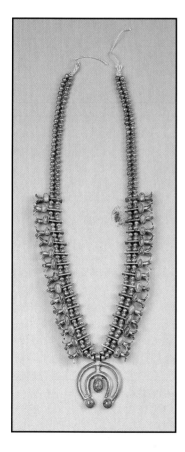

A silver necklace inlaid with turquoise stones. The "squash blossoms" charms on the neck strands and the central "naja" pendant are typical features of Navajo jewelry made in the 20th century.

This silver bird pendant measures only 1¼″ by 2″. Blue turquoise is used to represent the animal's eye and stomach.

A cast-silver bracelet decorated with geometric stamped designs and five polished turquoise stones.

A wrist guard made of leather and silver inset with turquoise and porcelain. Navajo bowmen traditionally wore wrist guards to protect their arms from bowstrings.

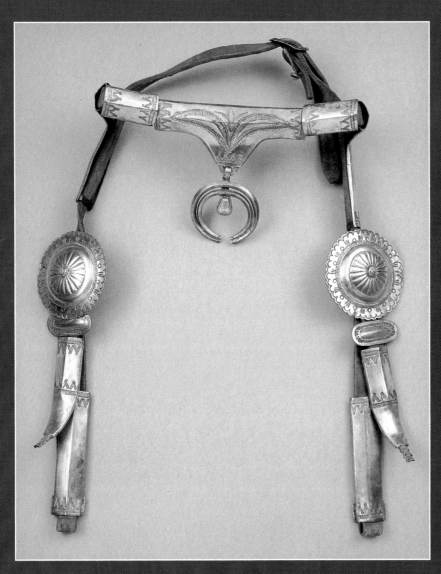

A silver headstall for a horse. The two discs (conchas) rested on the animal's cheeks, and the naja pendant rested on its forehead.

A belt made from seven silver conchas strung on a strap of leather.

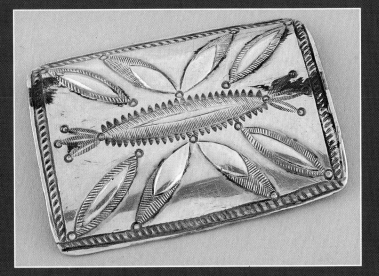

A silver belt buckle decorated with etched designs.

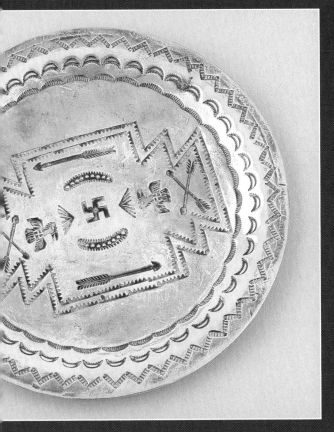

A silver tray with stamped designs. The Navajos often decorate objects sold to tourists with images that are not traditional but are perceived as "Indian" by whites.

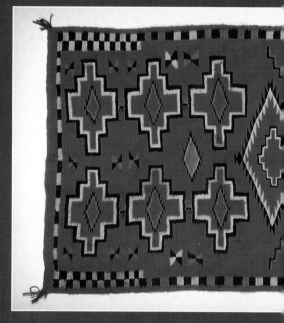

A 20th-century Navajo rug made with commercial dyes. Non-Indian customers often prefer the bright colors produced by artificial pigments.

A serape made between 1850 and 1875, the Classic Period of Navajo weaving.

This serape was woven in the Transitional Period (1875–90), during which the Navajos adapted their weaving traditions to satisfy the demands of the tourist market.

The pattern of horizontal stripes on this "chief blanket" has long been a favorite of Navajo weavers.

A woven saddlebag decorated with tassels, probably made in the early 20th century.

continued from page 64

land, the appropriation of federal funds to buy more land for tribes, and the establishment of a system of federal loans for tribal economic development. Perhaps most important, it allowed tribes, if they desired, to adopt formal constitutions and thereby give their tribal governments more legitimacy in their dealings with the BIA. Many Navajos, including Chee Dodge, wanted the Navajos to have a constitution because they wanted a stronger tribal council. But the very fact that Collier supported the IRA made many others suspicious. When the entire tribe's vote was counted, the Navajos had rejected the IRA's provisions. To this day the Navajos do not have a constitution, though some people have recently argued the need for one to increase federal government responsiveness and ensure the rights of Navajo individuals.

Other programs supported by Collier met with Navajo opposition for the same reason: guilt by association. The commissioner had been a severe critic of the off-reservation Indian boarding schools that had been operated by the federal government for more than 50 years. These institutions separated children not only from their parents but also from their culture. Collier instead favored day schools, from which children could return to their family each evening. He also wanted day schools to educate Indian students about their history and traditions, including their native language.

Many day schools were established in the 1930s on the Navajo reservation. Some of the teaching methods advocated by Collier would later be accepted by the Navajo people. Yet when the schools first opened, many Navajos spoke out against them. They were suspicious because day schools were a new idea and because they were linked with the unpopular John Collier.

During the late 1930s, the Navajo government underwent a number of changes at the direction of the BIA. In 1935, the six administrative divisions of the reservation were combined into a single agency, with its headquarters at Window Rock, Arizona. This agency was overseen by a single agent. The first to hold the office was E. Reesman Fryer, who was especially interested in carrying out the BIA's program for soil erosion control.

In 1938, the U.S. secretary of the interior established new regulations for the Navajo Tribal Council itself. Henceforth a much larger number of delegates (initially 74, but increasing with the population) were to be elected for 4-year terms by popular vote of the Navajo people. Other positions included a tribal chairman, a vice-chairman, and an executive committee chosen by the delegates.

As the tribal government changed, so too did the Navajo economy under the rigors of livestock reduction. With many people's herds now radically diminished, they could no longer depend upon raising livestock for their livelihood. The BIA tried to compensate by making federal public-works jobs available, but those Navajos who had suf-

A 1939 photograph of horses on the Navajo reservation. Thousands of sheep, cattle, and horses owned by Navajos were killed by government agents in the 1930s and 1940s as part of a compulsory livestock-reduction program, intended to halt soil erosion.

fered most from the reduction program were not always the ones who found work.

In some ways, the warnings of Chee Dodge to the U.S. Senate Committee on Indian Affairs seemed to have been accurate. Dodge had cautioned the committee during a public hearing in 1936:

> You take sheep away from a Navajo, that's all he knows. He isn't going to farm or anything like that; you might give a few acres to the poor ones, but stock-raising is in their heart. That's their work. If you keep on cutting down sheep, after a while the government will have to feed these people, give them rations; you know what that will cost.

Once reduction had fully taken effect on the reservation, a great many Navajos continued to live off the land, but gradually more began to seek work for wages in the small towns on the reservation and in the larger cities just beyond the borders of Navajo country. Some found jobs in railroad construction. Others worked as domestic servants, restaurant workers, or in similar service positions. At first the number of wageworkers was merely a trickle, but job seeking would become increasingly common by the late 1940s.

Such economic changes naturally had an impact on Navajo society. Extended families were affected by the absence of family members working off reservation. This in turn disrupted the traditional way of rearing children as well as customary relations among family members. The inability of traditional religious leaders to restore the balance of the Navajo world led some Navajos to consider alternatives or additions to their old religious practices. Some became more active within the various Christian churches. Others turned to a faith already established among many other tribes, the Native American Church.

The Native American Church combines elements of Christianity with rituals of traditional Indian religions. The most controversial aspect of the church—especially among the Navajos

Federal agents seize and corral Navajo horses before sending them to slaughter in 1940.

of the 1940s—was its ritual use of the peyote button, an outgrowth of the mescal cactus native to Mexico and the Southwest. Peyote buttons contain the drug mescaline and other substances that commonly induce hallucinations when ingested. For members of the Native American Church, the chewing of peyote buttons during religious rites is a means of communicating with God, and participation in the church helps them reaffirm their cultural identity and deal with life's difficulties. Some Na-

vajos, however, opposed the Native American Church because its beliefs and practices differed from the tribe's traditions. In 1940, the Navajo Tribal Council passed a resolution outlawing the use or possession of peyote, and tribal police sometimes arrested church members on such charges.

Although some members of the council were strongly criticized for their willingness to sanction the arrest of fellow tribe members and for their apparent cooperation in the livestock

Jacob Morgan, an opponent of reduction, at his inauguration as tribal chairman in 1938.

Chee Dodge, the first chairman of the Navajo Tribal Council, photographed in 1945 at the age of 85. Dodge was one of the Navajos' most influential leaders throughout the first half of the 20th century.

reduction program, the council became increasingly important throughout the 1930s. Like the Long Walk nearly 80 years earlier, the calamity of the reduction program had brought the Navajos together. To avoid future persecution, the Navajos now understood that they had to create a strong, independent government of their own—one that would benefit the people. As they mulled over how to proceed, their lives were suddenly and dramatically altered by the United States's involvement in World War II. ▲

Dr. Samuel Billison, a former president of the Navajo Codetalkers Association, speaking in Phoenix, Arizona, at the 1989 dedication of a statue representing a Navajo Codetalker.

THE
MODERN NAVAJO ERA
BEGINS

Some non-Indian Americans are surprised to learn that the Navajos played a vital role in helping the United States emerge victorious in World War II. They cannot understand why so many Navajos enlisted and fought for the United States, when Indians had so often been mistreated by the government and disparaged by non-Indian individuals. Certainly the era of livestock reduction had embittered many Navajos toward federal authority. Yet an impressive number saw themselves as both Navajo and American and wanted to become involved in the war effort. When the Japanese bombed Pearl Harbor, Hawaii, in December 1941, these Navajos felt it was their country that had been attacked and wanted to defend it.

In the Pacific theater of military operations, Navajo soldiers contributed a remarkable chapter to their people's proud history. At the battlefront, the American armed forces needed a code to send messages that the Japanese could not easily decipher. Phillip Johnston, the son of a missionary who had lived in Navajo country, came up with a plan. He suggested that the Navajo language serve as the basis for a code. The Marine Corps approved his idea and recruited several hundred Navajo men, who became known as the Navajo Codetalkers.

The Codetalkers proved very effective at their job. When the Marines landed on Japanese-held islands such as Iwo Jima, Guam, and Tarawa, the Codetalkers were in the front lines, establishing communication posts. Using code words and phrases (such as "sparrow hawk" for "dive bomber"), they could converse much more rapidly than anyone using an invented language, and their Japanese adversaries never cracked the complex Navajo code.

Navajo men also fought in Europe against German and Italian forces, and Navajo women served in the Women's Army Corps. Before leaving home to join the military, Navajo men and women commonly took part in a variation of the ancient Blessingway ceremonies used to safeguard departing warriors. After they returned home, they took part in other ceremonies to restore hozho lost through their war-

time experiences and their contact with other cultures. Some veterans who had seen combat partook in a ceremony called the Enemyway, devised to protect warriors from the spirits of their slain enemies.

To this day older Navajos remember the World War II era with great emotion. About 3,600 served in the various branches of the military, and for many the war was their first exposure to the world outside the reservation. To the generation that lived through that time, the Codetalkers came to symbolize the

Privates J. W. Harding, J. D. Gatewood, and Billy Odell—3 of the more than 3,600 Navajos who served in the military during World War II.

Some Navajo civilians helped in the war effort by growing sugar beets, which were used as a substitute for cane sugar.

Navajo role in America's ordeal and ultimate triumph, and they were singled out for honors by both fellow Navajos and non-Indians. In 1989, for example, a large statue of a Codetalker was erected in Phoenix, Arizona.

On the reservation, money sent home by Navajo servicemen temporarily helped the tribe's suffering economy. Some Navajo civilians found work off reservation as factory workers and as field hands harvesting sugar beets, which were used as a substitute for imported cane sugar during the war. People also continued to make their living by traditional means, such as weaving, silversmithing, and farming. Livestock raising, however, was in de-

cline. The reduction program was carried out through the mid-1940s. After the program had been concluded, government officials collected statistics that showed that the average weight and wool production of Navajo sheep had increased. To support this conclusion, they had photographs of Navajo sheep before and after the program, observing how much healthier the animals in the latter appeared. The Navajos, of course, did not see it this way.

At the end of the war, the return of thousands of unemployed veterans to the reservation caused an economic crisis. It was impossible for the Navajos to prosper with a livestock-based economy, yet well-paid jobs off the reservation were out of reach to most because of their limited command of English and lack of education. The veterans, who had been immersed in the outside world, were convinced that Navajo society had to learn for its own good to deal more effectively with the non-Indian populace.

In addition to all these concerns, the Navajos and other groups were being confronted with a changing attitude among non-Indians toward traditional Indian ways of life. All Americans had worked together to win the war, putting differences aside for a common cause. Because Indians had played such a valiant role in achieving victory, many non-Indians concluded they deserved to be treated just like all other Americans. They argued that Indian communities should no longer be separated or segregated from the majority of the population.

This sentiment inspired a new federal Indian policy known as *termination*. This policy sought to terminate, or end, the federal government's financial responsibilities to tribes and gradually to withdraw its special protection of reservation lands. The individual state governments would then assume much of the responsibility for the well-being of the Indians within their boundaries. Advocates of termination felt it would "free" Indians to join mainstream American society.

But most Indians, including the Navajos, opposed termination, regarding it not as a reward but as a threat. They did not want to be treated just like

everyone else because they were *not* just like everyone else. They argued that Indians, as the original inhabitants of North America, had a unique history. Their ancestors had signed treaties and agreements with the federal government, and therefore they were entitled to the unique legal status these treaties granted them. Although tribes were not always pleased with the way in which the federal government acted toward them, they were even warier of state governments, most of which in the past had shown little interest in the Indians.

One of the earliest instruments of termination policy was the Indian Claims Commission (ICC), which was authorized by Congress in 1946. The ICC established a temporary federal court in which tribes could sue the federal government for lost land and other damages. Resolution of, and compensation for, these claims was to be a preliminary step in ending the federal government's financial obligation to Indian groups.

Before the Navajos could sue the government, they needed legal assistance, and they had never before employed a lawyer or law firm to represent them. One of the first acts of tribal chairman Sam Ahkeah, who was elected in 1946, was to hire Norman Littell, a former U.S. assistant attorney general. Littell took on the job as the Navajos' attorney in addition to his partnership in a Washington, D.C., law firm.

Littell was a bright and forceful man who left a major imprint on the Navajo people. During the nearly 20 years Littell acted as their lawyer, he encouraged the Navajos to develop their political institutions and generally look out for their own economic and legal interests. He advised the tribal council, represented the Navajos in various cases, and was a vital force in the tribal capital of Window Rock, Arizona, for a generation. During Littell's years as the Navajos' attorney, he encouraged the tribal council to meet more often and take a more aggressive stance toward non-Indian-owned businesses on the reservations.

In 1947, Sam Ahkeah also took up residence in Window Rock, and the tribal council instituted an executive committee, also called an advisory committee, to consider important local issues. Over the next few years, Ahkeah and other prominent Navajos, such as Jacob Morgan, testified before Congress about the urgent need for improved roads, schools, health care, and other concerns.

Congress responded by passing the Navajo-Hopi Rehabilitation Act of 1950. This legislation was in keeping with the termination era, for it was designed to

A caravan of U.S. Army and BIA workers in Black Mountain, Arizona, bringing emergency medical care and supplies to Navajos trapped in isolated areas of the reservation following a 1949 snowstorm. Such occurrences led the Navajo Tribal Council in the 1950s to allocate millions of dollars to the improvement of reservation roads.

A classroom in a school for Navajo children, run by the Bureau of Indian Affairs. Although the federal government increased funding for the establishment of reservation day schools in the 1950s, many Navajo students in remote areas still had to enroll in boarding schools far from home.

encourage the Navajos to take charge of their own economic development. Through this act, the tribe received $88 million over a 10-year period for internal projects. Almost $25 million was spent to construct schools, but even more was directed toward improving reservation roads and highways.

New and improved roads and highways gave the Navajos greater choice as to where they worked and shopped. Suddenly there were alternatives to the nearest trading post. As driving conditions improved, more tourists came to Navajo country, and after World War II tourism sharply boosted the tribal economy. The development of industries on the reservations, a goal strongly encouraged by the federal government, appeared feasible as road travel became easier. And, for better or worse, the isolation of most rural residents of the reservation was reduced. Although many communities were still difficult to reach, especially in the snowy winter months, a basic change had occurred in Navajo life.

Improved roads also allowed Navajo children more access to schools. If they were to survive and prosper, the Navajos knew, their children and young adults needed better education. Returning veterans had come home to find that the majority of children on the reservation were not enrolled in school. In years past, children had been needed to help care for the sheep herds. But with an increasing number of adults becoming wageworkers, younger Navajos now had the time to attend school. New educational programs and new institutions had to be started quickly.

For the younger students, several alternatives existed. Some attended existing BIA or mission schools on the reservation, but there were too few of these institutions to accommodate all school-age Navajo children. During the 1950s, the BIA funded 36 temporary schools, housed in trailers and scattered across the reservation. These gradually enrolled more than a thousand elementary school students. Yet even with these temporary schools, thousands of Navajo children—especially those over elementary-school age—had to board away from home. A few students attended existing BIA boarding schools off reservation. During the 1950s, the tribal government also constructed student dormitories near towns just outside the Navajo reservation, such as Gallup, New Mexico, and Flagstaff, Arizona; some teenage Navajo students lived in these and attended the towns' non-Indian public high schools. But Navajo parents became more involved in their children's education, and they demanded more local schools.

The obvious answer was to develop a public school system on the reservation. But public schools are usually funded by state governments using state tax revenues. The residents of federal Indian reservations, however, are exempt from state and local taxes. Because the Navajos did not pay property tax to Arizona, New Mexico, and Utah, the three states over which the reservation spread, these states' governments were unwilling to build and run reservation schools. Another source of funding had to be found.

In 1950, Congress passed two laws authorizing federal aid to public school districts that educated the children of military personnel. Three years later, these laws were amended to finance the construction and operation of schools on Indian reservations as well. This federal funding made it possible for the Navajos in the 1950s to begin to build the core of a public school system inside the reservation boundaries. For the first time thousands of Navajo children were able to attend school and still return home to their families at night. But even after a nucleus of about 20 schools was completed, many students living in the most remote areas of the reservation were still forced by distance to attend boarding schools.

An oil-pumping station at Four Corners, on the Navajo reservation, in 1962. Oil royalties bring millions of dollars into the tribal treasury annually.

The Navajos also made efforts to improve educational opportunities for young adults who had not attended school as children. In 1946, a special five-year program was created by the BIA for students too old to take classes at the early elementary level. Off-reservation boarding schools—such as the Sherman Institute in Riverside, California, and the Intermountain School in Brigham City, Utah—also enrolled many older Navajo students. These schools offered instruction in English and vocational training in such skills as welding, auto mechanics, and upholstering.

Most of the money for these programs came from the U.S. government, but another source of funds was found in the mid-1950s when natural resources were again discovered on Navajo lands. Oil companies renewed their interest in the region, and in 1956–57 large oil and gas fields were found on the reservation near an area called Four Corners, where the borders of Arizona, New Mexico, Colorado, and Utah meet. This discovery was a great boom to the Navajo economy. Navajo oil royalties soon ran into the millions of dollars each year. With these funds coming in to the tribal treasury, the council began to think more ambitiously about funding its own institutions.

Money from newly exploited uranium deposits also added to the tribal funds. During World War II an enterprise called the Vanadium Corporation had begun mining uranium on reservation lands. Interest in atomic energy grew rapidly after the war, and consequently so did Navajo revenues. In 1950, the tribe earned $65,000 in uranium money; in 1954, the amount had increased tenfold—to $650,000. At the same time the tribe was also earning money by carefully managing its own lumber industry.

In 1969, through a tribal council resolution, the Navajos would begin officially to call themselves the Navajo Nation. That resolution was able to come about because of the development born in the 1950s, a decade when the Navajos at last possessed both the financial resources and the determination to take charge of their destiny. In

A Navajo Forest Products Industry truck collecting lumber. The development of the tribal lumber industry in the late 1950s helped to boost the Navajo economy.

the face of federal and public efforts to assimilate the Navajos, the people grew all the more determined to assert their dual identity as Navajo Americans.

During the 1950s, through the leadership of tribal chairman Sam Ahkeah and his successor Paul Jones and the hard work of many others, the Navajos made numerous other significant improvements in reservation life. New chapter houses were built. A tribal college-scholarship program was created. The court system was revamped and the council was given power to appoint seven judges for life terms. The tribal government was expanded to deal with wider responsibilities. The *Navajo Times*, a reservationwide newspaper written in English, was established. In 1958, a tribal sawmill became the basis of the Navajo Forest Products Industries (NFPI), and the following year the Navajo Tribal Utilities Authority (NTUA) was founded. Despite the many challenges the Navajos faced by the end of the 1950s, they had built a solid foundation on which to construct their new nation. ▲

Tribal chairman Peter MacDonald behind his desk at the Navajo cap-
ital of Window Rock, Arizona, in 1979.

THE
NAVAJO NATION

The 1960s, 1970s, and 1980s have been an extraordinary period in Navajo history, an era marked by optimism and confusion, cohesion and controversy. Through it all, the Navajos have clearly emerged as major participants in southwestern society and in national American Indian life. Since 1960, the Navajo population has doubled, soaring to about 200,000. The tribe remains the largest in the United States and occupies more than 25,000 square miles of land. Despite progressive innovations in such areas as legal aid, health care, and industry, many ancient cultural traditions remain lively. Yet troubling questions about the Navajos' future remain.

Navajo education is one sphere that has seen enormous development. By the mid-1960s, four types of schools existed in Navajo country: mission schools, BIA boarding and day schools, public schools, and contract schools. The last of these were run by employees hired by locally elected school boards that were granted at least partial funding for these institutions through contracts with the BIA.

Over the course of the 1960s, the BIA's direct role in Navajo education declined. On-reservation boarding schools served primarily students from the reservation's most remote areas. During the end of the decade, the BIA did open new elementary boarding schools in the Arizona communities of Chuska, Toyei, and Many Farms, and new boarding high schools in Many Farms and Tuba City. At the same time, however, it closed some older, smaller schools. On the whole, the percentage of Navajos attending BIA schools decreased. Off-reservation boarding high schools, which had at one time enrolled hundreds of students, were nearly all shut down.

The Navajos' dissatisfaction with BIA schools, especially boarding schools that cut children off from their parents and community, led to the push for contract schools. Although these were dependent largely on the BIA for funding, the Navajos had greater control over what was taught in their classrooms. The Navajos' first contract school was Rough Rock Demonstration School, which opened in 1966.

Rough Rock, an isolated community in the heart of Navajo country, proved an ideal location for this pioneering venture. Although the local school board members themselves had little formal education, they were well known and respected in the community, which gave the school great support. Most Rough Rock residents were traditionalists who raised sheep, traded at the local post, and spoke Navajo as their first language.

The board hired Robert Roessel, the white husband of a Navajo woman, as Rough Rock Demonstration School's first principal, and he in turn hired its teaching staff. Roessel had taught for many years in various Navajo schools, and under his charismatic leadership the school at Rough Rock quickly gained national attention. Native history, culture, and language received much more emphasis at the new school than in any BIA institution. In the fall of 1968, Roessel relinquished his post to a Navajo, Dillon Platero.

Rough Rock Demonstration School soon served as a model for similar institutions in other communities, such as Rock Point School in Arizona and Ramah School and Borrego Pass School in New Mexico. The Rough Rock school's Navajo Curriculum Center proved particularly influential. The center published and distributed innovative educational materials such as primers written in both Navajo and English, employing traditional stories and examples drawn from Navajo life. Using these, teachers encouraged students not only to speak Navajo but to learn how to read and write it.

In the 1960s and 1970s, following the example of the relatively few contract schools, many state-run public schools departed from their old goal of completely integrating Navajo students into the mainstream culture. At this time, more and more Navajo children began to attend public schools, thanks to improved roads and the relocation of many families into towns or their environs, where wagework could be found. In turn, more Navajos gradually registered to vote and elected increasing numbers of Navajo school board members, who insisted on new school policies that were more in keeping with Navajo values. Navajo parents were, of course, as divided as any group of non-Indian parents about what constituted the best schooling for their children. But as parental involvement in schools increased, so did the quality of elementary and secondary education available to all Navajo students.

Increased Navajo control did not, however, in itself solve some deep-rooted problems of their educational system. Low salaries, frequent turnover of personnel, and student dropout rates higher than the national average remained serious concerns. Nevertheless, more Navajos became teachers and administrators at reservation schools, which gave Navajo children role models whom they could respect and emulate.

With help from the tribal scholarship fund and other grants, loans, and programs, record numbers of Navajos began to attend colleges and universities. These included the state universities of Arizona, New Mexico, and Utah, as well as private institutions such as Brigham Young University in Provo, Utah. Many graduates have returned home to work as lawyers, teachers, or professionals trained in other areas.

Because not every deserving Navajo student was able to leave the reservation, the tribal council in 1968 founded the Navajo Community College (NCC)—the first community college established on any Indian reservation. Originally located at Many Farms, NCC's permanent campus opened in 1973 at Tsaile, Arizona, and a branch campus opened later at Shiprock, New Mexico. The college, which graduated its first students in 1970, offers associate degrees based on two-year programs; one degree, for example, is in bilingual-bicultural education. Courses are also taught in traditional subjects such as

A Navajo student learns about Spider Woman, a figure in tribal lore. Such myths now have a prominent place in modern Navajo education.

weaving, and NCC's arts and crafts program now produces skilled silversmiths as well.

In 1972, the United Presbyterian church founded a second on-reservation postsecondary institution, the College of Ganado, at Ganado, Arizona. This school, like NCC, offered two-year programs toward an associate degree, but it stressed a more conventional curriculum. Some students from the Hopi and other southwestern Indian reservations also attended Ganado. A number of Ganado and NCC students have gone on to receive a bachelor's degree from a four-year university, but in September 1986 Ganado itself—never a very large school—closed its doors for lack of funds and students. However, NCC immediately moved to convert

The Ned A. Hatathli Culture Center on the Navajo Community College campus, photographed in 1979.

part of the Ganado campus to its own use.

Just as education boomed in the 1960s and 1970s, legal representation became more available to Navajos at this time. In the late 1950s, legal help was first offered to Navajo individuals by several Legal Aid Service lawyers hired by the tribe. But there were too few lawyers to meet the people's overwhelming needs.

In 1963, Lyndon B. Johnson became president and soon announced that the federal government would wage a "war on poverty" in the United States. As part of this program, the Johnson administration created the Office of Economic Opportunity (OEO) in Washington, D.C. Funds from the OEO

helped to establish the Office of Navajo Economic Opportunity (ONEO) on the Navajo reservation. One of ONEO's most popular programs was its legal service, which was popularly dubbed Dinebeiina Nahiilna be Agitahe (Navajo for "attorneys who contribute to the economic revitalization of the people") and soon shortened to DNA.

DNA rapidly hired 18 law school graduates, opened offices in several towns, and took on a variety of cases. These dealt with workmen's compensation claims, landlord-tenant problems, divorce suits, misdemeanor offenses, grazing rights disputes, and more. Given DNA's willingness to confront controversial issues, it appeared doomed in its first years. But because it helped so many people, it proved impossible to get rid of.

Federal funding of DNA and its parent was part of a new national policy toward American Indian groups. Called self-determination, it sought to encourage tribes to take control of their own economic well-being by funding programs to promote economic growth on reservations. Among other ONEO ventures at this time were the establishment of a small-business development center, an extensive preschool teaching program, a recreation program, a Neighborhood Youth Corps (which involved thousands of teens), and a Home Improvement Training program. Millions of dollars of federal money were allocated to these programs, and Navajos soon filled most of ONEO's administrative positions. Heading ONEO was a man who has since dominated Navajo political life for more than a generation, Peter MacDonald.

Born December 16, 1928, in the reservation community of Teec Nos Pos, Arizona, MacDonald grew up speaking Navajo and learning traditional ways. As a teenager he enlisted in the Marine Corps and became one of the youngest Codetalkers. After World War II, he resumed his education at Bacone High School in Oklahoma. In 1957 he earned a B.S. in electrical engineering from the University of Oklahoma. MacDonald worked for six years as a project engineer with Hughes Aircraft in southern California. In 1963, he returned to the Navajo reservation and gained a position with the tribal government. After

helping to draft some Navajo management plans and a successful request for federal funds, he became—by a tribal board appointment—director of ONEO in May 1965.

In this position, MacDonald quickly assumed center stage in the drama of Navajo public life. For five years MacDonald directed, with high visibility, heavily funded programs such as DNA that had a widespread impact on the Navajo Nation. People soon came to associate him with these generous, Navajo-run efforts. In 1970, MacDonald resigned from ONEO to run for tribal chairman against incumbent Raymond Nakai.

Tribal chairman Raymond Nakai in 1968, holding a proclamation of the 100th anniversary of the establishment of the Navajo Indian Reservation.

MacDonald's assets included familiarity with federal funding methods, a traditional background combined with off-reservation experience, and a history of close contact with the Navajo people while heading ONEO. Nakai emphasized to voters his achievements as tribal chairman, including improved education, purchases of new land for the reservation, and the establishment of new industry.

How best to develop industry without depleting Navajo resources or disrupting traditional ways was an important question during the election. Expansion of the Navajo economy had been a perennial challenge to the tribal council and chairman. Most Navajos did not want to leave their homeland. Yet job prospects were limited, especially for those with little education or training. Livestock raising, agriculture, tourism, and traditional crafts would support only a limited number of people. The tribal government itself, local schools, and federal government agencies all offered employment to those qualified, but clearly greater opportunities were needed. The reservation's geographic isolation and the scarcity of seed money had long deterred local residents from starting new businesses. Consequently, in the early 1960s the Navajos had decided to try to take better advantage of the reservation's natural resources. They tried to persuade non-Indian-owned, well-capitalized companies to come onto the reservation and not only pay for whatever

resources they used but also train and employ Navajos.

At the start of the 1960s, oil revenue continued to inflate the tribal treasury. But coal and uranium mining also became major new sources of income. The rapidly growing population of California and the Southwest had created a market for these fuels. The developing regional economy desperately needed new energy sources.

In 1962, Utah Mining and Manufacturing signed a contract with the Navajos that allowed them to strip-mine coal from land south of the San Juan River in New Mexico. Adjacent to this land, the Arizona Public Service Company constructed an electricity-generating facility, the Four Corners Power Plant. Later, in 1964 and 1966, the tribal council also agreed to lease lands on Black Mesa for strip mining by the Peabody Coal Company and to allow a power plant to be built at Page, Arizona. All these agreements were negotiated by Chairman Nakai and the council to boost the tribal funds and create jobs. At the time, however, most council members did not fully realize how much damage strip mining and coal-fired plants could cause.

Strip mining involves the removal of successive layers of earth from a vast expanse of land to get at the mineral deposits underneath. Once the deposits are exhausted, only a vast, barren open pit remains. The refining of the raw deposits also requires large quantities of water, a scarce resource in Navajo country. Finally, the burning of the refined coal itself at the power plants generates an alarming amount of air pollution. Aside from a concern for the damage this did to the tourist industry, many Navajos also agonized that they were selling their very birthright for a short-term gain. They feared that after the resources—and the companies that needed them—were gone, their land would be forever destroyed.

But these increasingly controversial, resource-depleting enterprises were not the only ones to locate on Navajo land during the Nakai administration. The Navajos sought to lure other large-scale industry with cheap land leases, favorable construction arrangements, and a trainable work force. Two major firms accepted the Navajos' invitation: Fairchild Semiconductor and the General Dynamics Corporation. These manufacturing concerns, however, yielded fewer jobs and less tribal income than the people had initially hoped.

Strip-mining operations near Window Rock, the capital of the Navajo reservation. During Raymond Nakai's administration, many Navajos began to object to the council's leasing of land to mining companies because of the environmental damage caused by strip mining.

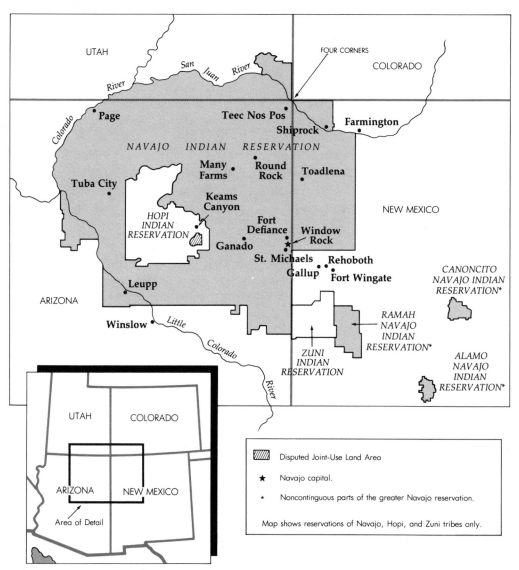

Another major concern at the time of the Nakai-MacDonald contest was the joint-use land area shared with the Hopi tribe, whose own reservation was entirely surrounded by that of the Navajos. Problems over the joint-use area dated back to the original 1882 executive order; they had grown of increasing concern to the Navajos as questions arose not simply over grazing rights but also over mineral and even occupancy rights. When the Hopis won exclusive occupancy rights in a court case, Navajos regarded the decision as a major defeat, and longtime tribal attorney Norman Littell was ousted not long thereafter. MacDonald charged Nakai's new tribal attorney, Harold Mott, with being inexperienced in Indian law and exceeding his authority.

In the election of November 1970, MacDonald received nearly three votes to every one cast for Nakai. In his inaugural address the following January, the new tribal chairman pledged:

> What is rightfully ours, we must protect; what is rightfully due us we must claim. . . . What we depend on from others, we must replace with the labor of our own hands and the skills of our own people. . . . What we do not have, we must bring into being. We must create for ourselves.

MacDonald pledged not to "barter away the Navajo birthright for quick profit" and further argued that the tribe must no longer "depend on others to run our schools, build our roads, administer our health programs, construct our houses, manage our industries."

The Navajo government under the MacDonald administration promptly took on a more aggressive attitude. At the chairman's urging, the Navajos hired new legal counsel, the Phoenix-based firm of Brown, Vlassis and Bain. One partner, George Vlassis, served as the tribe's primary attorney. In 1971, the tribal council created a Navajo Division of Education, which subse-

quently started a teacher education program to increase the number of Navajo instructors. The next year the Navajo Housing Authority was formed to build and manage tribal housing with money from the U.S. Department of Housing and Urban Development (HUD). At MacDonald's invitation, the AFL-CIO labor union federation set up a worker training program that helped decrease tribal unemployment. Voter registration drives boosted the Navajos' political clout, especially in Arizona, forcing non-Indian politicians to pay attention to local interests. Finally, MacDonald instituted the renegotiation of old gas and oil leases on terms more profitable to the Navajos.

The tribe's economic problems were not easily solved, however. In the 1970s, an attempt to develop Navajo uranium resources resulted in protests that echoed those made earlier against coal extraction. In a joint venture that made the Navajos partners rather than employees, Exxon agreed to pay the tribe $6 million for uranium exploration rights in northwestern New Mexico. The Navajos hoped to gain millions more from the actual operations. But once again controversy erupted. Local residents complained bitterly that they had not been consulted. Concerns escalated as reports surfaced about the poor health of Navajo uranium miners who had worked in the area of Grants, New Mexico. The highly publicized closing in 1979 of the Three Mile Island nuclear power plant near Harrisburg, Pennsylvania, caused further worries about the safety of nuclear power. Such concerns, combined with plummeting market prices for uranium ore, left the proposed joint venture in oblivion as of the late 1980s.

During most of this period the Navajo Forest Products Industries (NFPI) had a more positive image. Based in the community of Navajo, New Mexico, NFPI represented Navajo control and careful management of the tribe's forests. By the late 1970s it had more than 600 Navajos on its payroll and indirectly employed hundreds more. A falling timber market nationally would present new problems for the operation in the 1980s, but generally NFPI's record reflected a successful use of this resource, which—unlike oil and coal—was both "clean" and renewable.

Unfortunately, another effort modeled after NFPI proved less productive. The Navajo Agricultural Products Industry (NAPI) had been created in April 1970 to operate a 100,000-acre farm. This land was to be irrigated as part of the Navajo Indian Irrigation Project, which had long promised to deliver water to the Navajos from the San Juan River in New Mexico. Although the participants—including Bahe Billy, a Navajo agriculturalist who had earned his doctorate at the University of Arizona—were dedicated to making NAPI work, the project was often mismanaged and suffered major financial setbacks. Disputes also arose from allegations that some individuals were being allowed access to NAPI land because of their influence in reservation

politics. Because of these problems, only part of this land is currently irrigated.

Such disputes are indicative of the greater problem of uncertain water rights, a severe drawback to economic development on the reservation. In theory, the Navajos possess important water rights, but in practice they have exercised very little of this potential power. The Colorado River and other sources of water are already oversubscribed. A court victory by the Navajos could represent a crucial breakthrough, but in a region where little rain falls, the Navajos face formidable non-Indian competition for this particularly precious resource.

Throughout his campaign against Raymond Nakai and his first term in office, MacDonald had repeatedly sounded the theme of Navajo self-determination. He contended that Navajos needed to open more of their own businesses so that they could stop relying so heavily on wages from non-Indian employers and welfare from the government. Navajo entrepreneurs responded to his call by establishing small businesses. Gas stations that are owned or leased by Navajos now dot the reservation. One Navajo man, Don Davis, opened a Chevrolet dealership in Tuba City, Arizona, in December 1978. The tribal government also continued to promote tourism with enthusiasm. Canyon de Chelly, Monument Valley, and other natural wonders attracted growing numbers of foreign and American visitors.

A number of communities also established cooperative businesses. An early example was the Pinon Co-op. It was founded in 1971 in Pinon, Arizona, partly as an alternative to trading posts, which continued to be run largely by non-Indians. The Pinon Co-op sold groceries, gasoline, and dry goods, and subsequent cooperative ventures offered feed for livestock as well. Credit unions and arts and crafts cooperatives also provided Navajos with the opportunity for community-based, mutually beneficial endeavors.

During his first term, MacDonald appeared to provide bold new leadership for the Navajos. He challenged them to raise their ambitions and to develop a more assertive posture in dealing with the reservation's non-Indian neighbors. He outlined goals for the future and projected confidence that the people could meet these goals. In 1974, MacDonald won reelection by a comfortable margin.

By the early part of his second term, however, the chairman had lost the solid support he once enjoyed. His critics charged that, despite MacDonald's rhetoric of self-determination, the Navajos' situation had not actually changed. In 1975, the reservation suf-

These three Navajo homes, photographed in 1967 outside of Farmington, New Mexico, demonstrate how old and new ways coexist in the modern Navajo Nation.

Two Navajo protesters negotiating with an employee of Fairchild Semiconductor in 1975. Activists, including members of the American Indian Movement, seized the company's plant at Shiprock after it laid off a number of local employees due to a recession.

fered a disturbing, though relatively minor, fiscal setback after Fairchild Semiconductor cut employment at its reservation plant because of a nationwide economic recession. When members of the American Indian Movement (AIM), a militant political group, seized the plant in protest, Fairchild responded by shutting down the long-ailing plant—permanently.

More damaging to MacDonald was a scandal that wracked the Navajo Housing Authority (NHA). In February 1976, Arizona senator Barry Goldwater demanded a federal audit of the tribal government, following rumors of corruption. An NHA official ultimately pleaded guilty to charges involving misuse of more than $13 million in housing funds. In 1977, MacDonald himself was indicted by a Phoenix grand jury on the allegation that he had submitted false invoices to a utility company. The chairman hired criminal lawyer F. Lee Bailey for his defense, and the jury was unable to reach a verdict on the eight federal charges against him.

Despite the damaging publicity that resulted, MacDonald was reelected in 1978, again by a three-to-one margin, because the other candidates split the votes of those who opposed him. His election to three consecutive terms was unprecedented in Navajo politics. Indeed, MacDonald looked unbeatable at the polls until four years later, when a candidate of comparable stature entered the race for the chairmanship. In Peterson Zah, director of DNA, MacDonald finally faced a rival who ran the type of campaign he himself had waged against incumbent Raymond Nakai in 1970. Zah defeated MacDonald and served as tribal chairman from 1982 to 1986.

Originally from Low Mountain, Arizona, and a graduate of Arizona State University, Zah at first seemed capable of holding on to the chairmanship for more than a single term. But MacDonald retained a considerable following in certain chapters, and events seemed to conspire against Zah's success. Perhaps foremost among these was the continuing land dispute between the Navajos and the Hopis. A judicial decision proclaimed that Navajos living in the contested area were to be relocated elsewhere. Although the number of residents to be removed was reduced in subsequent haggling, as was

Navajo women weeping as they are forced to relocate from their homes in Cactus Valley, Arizona, a disputed reservation area, in 1986. Disputes between the Hopi and Navajo tribes over occupancy rights continue to rage today.

the amount of acreage to be surrendered, the final result was widely seen as another Navajo loss. MacDonald's militant stance played well with the Navajo public, in contrast to Zah's moderate public tone. The chairman was also criticized for his inability to work out an agreement with his former schoolmate, Hopi tribal chairman Ivan Sidney. Zah's popularity suffered as

well from a general slowdown in the Navajo economy during his years in office. In actuality, this stemmed largely from cutbacks in federal aid that the tribe was powerless to prevent. Nonetheless, Zah bore the brunt of Navajo dissatisfaction over the recession.

As a result, the 1986 tribal election was a bitterly contested race. Peterson Zah actually carried three of the five

Navajo children, dressed in a mixture of traditional and mainstream garb, cruise in the back of a pickup truck, the preferred vehicle of many tribe members today.

Navajo electoral districts, but Peter MacDonald soundly defeated the incumbent elsewhere. When the votes were tallied, MacDonald had won election to a fourth term by a margin of 750 votes out of some 61,000 cast.

But Peter MacDonald's return to power was troubled from the very beginning. Within a month of taking office, the chairman ordered the *Navajo Times* closed down. His reasoning was that the newpaper was losing money, but his opponents claimed it was because the paper had been persistently critical of MacDonald. A few months later, the *Navajo Times* resumed publication on a weekly basis.

The chairman's troubles were just starting, however. In the middle of his fourth term of office, MacDonald became the center of political turmoil when, during hearings of the U.S. Senate Select Committee on Indian Affairs in January 1989, he was accused by Navajo and non-Navajo witnesses alike of receiving kickbacks—specifically, of benefiting personally from the tribal government's purchase of a ranch of nearly a half million acres south of the Grand Canyon. The tribal council soon placed its chairman on administrative leave; and the following month MacDonald conceded on KTNN Radio, a Navajo station in Window Rock, that he had indeed taken "gifts" from individuals seeking business deals with the reservation. "Yes, I have accepted gifts," he told listeners, according to a subsequent newspaper account. "But that is not a crime."

This revelation divided the Navajos into two factions. In the absence of a formal tribal constitution, both pro- and anti-MacDonald groups claimed control of the government. Ultimately, in an attempt at compromise and conciliation, the tribal council appointed an interim chairman to serve out the remainder of MacDonald's term: Leonard Haskie, a council member from Sanostee, New Mexico, who was comparatively unknown outside the Navajo reservation. Despite this appointment, political marches and demonstrations continued. In July 1989, two Navajo men were killed and several other people injured when a pro-McDonald rally erupted into a violent confrontation with Navajo tribal police. With this event, it became clear that, regardless of who eventually retained

government control, years would pass before the political shock waves died down.

Optimistic observers expressed the hope that the Navajos might at least emerge from this political struggle with a renewed sense of national purpose. But the Navajo Nation is far more than a political entity. It represents a unique people who together have survived the misery of the Long Walk, the confinement at Fort Sumner, and the trauma of livestock reduction. There can be no doubt that this people will endure.

As the Navajos prepare for the 21st century, they continue to blend change with continuity. A significant percentage of the people still speak the Navajo language, practice traditional ceremonies, and honor old values. A justifiably proud people with a rich heritage, they continue to gain strength from their home territory. Within the four sacred mountains the Navajos will try, as Barboncito foretold so many years ago, to remain as happy and as prosperous as the land. ▲

BIBLIOGRAPHY

Bailey, Garrick, and Roberta Glenn Bailey. *A History of the Navajos: The Reservation Years*. Sante Fe: School of American Research Press, 1986.

Bingham, Sam, and Janet Bingham, eds. *Between Sacred Mountains: Navajo Stories and Lessons from the Land*. Tucson: University of Arizona Press, 1984.

Correll, J. Lee. *Through White Men's Eyes: A Contribution to Navajo History (A Chronological Record of the Navajo People from Earliest Times to the Treaty of June 1, 1968)*. 6 vols. Window Rock, AZ: Navajo Heritage Center, 1979.

Iverson, Peter. *The Navajo Nation*. Albuquerque: University of New Mexico Press, 1983.

———. *The Navajos: A Critical Bibliography*. Bloomington: Indiana University Press, 1976.

Kluckholn, Clyde, and Dorothea Leighton. *The Navaho*. Garden City, NY: Natural History Library, 1962.

Ortiz, Alfonso, ed. *Handbook of North American Indians*. Vol. 10, *Southwest*, 393–400, 489–683. Washington, DC: Smithsonian Institution, 1983.

Reichard, Gladys. *Navaho Religion: A Study of Symbolism*. New York: Pantheon, 1950.

Roessel, Ruth, ed. *Navajo Stories of the Long Walk Period*. Tsaile, AZ: Navajo Community College Press, 1973.

Underhill, Ruth. *The Navajos*. Norman: University of Oklahoma Press, 1967.

Witherspoon, Gary. *Language and Art in the Navajo Universe*. Ann Arbor: University of Michigan Press, 1977.

Yazzie, Ethelou, ed. *Navajo History*. Vol. 1. Many Farms, AZ: Navajo Community College Press for the Navajo Curriculum Center, Rough Rock Demonstration School, 1971.

THE NAVAJOS AT A GLANCE

TRIBE *Navajos*

CULTURE AREA *Southwest*

GEOGRAPHY *Colorado plateau country of northeastern Arizona,*
northwestern New Mexico, and southeastern Utah

LINGUISTIC FAMILY *Athapaskan*

CURRENT POPULATION *Approximately 200,000*

FIRST CONTACT *Probably Antonio de Espejo, Spanish, 1582*

FEDERAL STATUS *Recognized. The Navajo Indian Reservation*
includes approximately 32,000 square miles of
land. It is located primarily in Arizona and
extends into New Mexico and Utah.

GLOSSARY

agriculture The science, art, and business of soil cultivation, crop production, and the raising of livestock.

anthropology The study of the origin and the physical, social, and cultural development and behavior of humans.

archaeology The recovery and study of evidence of human ways of life, especially that of prehistoric peoples but also including that of historic peoples.

assimilation The absorption of a culturally distinct group into the prevailing culture.

Athapaskan languages A group of related languages spoken by Indian peoples whose ancestors were native to the region of Lake Athapaska in northwestern Canada. Among the languages in this group are those of the Navajos, the Hupa, and the Mescalero Apaches.

barter Trade without the exchange of money.

Blessingway rite The core ritual of the Navajos' traditional religion. Variations of this ceremony can be performed for any number of purposes including the protection of livestock, the blessing of a marriage, or the protection of warriors from their enemies.

Bureau of Indian Affairs (BIA) A U.S. government agency established in 1824 and assigned to the Department of the Interior in 1849. Originally intended to manage trade and other relations with Indians and especially to supervise tribes on reservations, the BIA is now involved in programs to encourage Indians to manage their own affairs and improve their educational opportunities and general social and economic well-being.

chantways Navajo rituals performed to heal or protect a person, presided over by a singer who fulfills the functions of both doctor and priest.

clan A multigenerational group that has in common their identity, organization, and property and that claims descent from a common ancestor. Because clan members consider themselves closely related, marriage within the clan is strictly prohibited.

Codetalkers A group of several hundred Navajo men who were selected by the Marine Corps during World War II to send coded messages to Pacific battlefronts. The Navajo language served as the basis for the code, which was instrumental in defeating the Japanese.

culture The learned behavior of human beings; nonbiological, socially taught activities; the way of life of a given group of people.

Diné The Navajo word meaning "The People." This is the term the Navajos use to refer to themselves.

Dinétah The Navajo word meaning "The Land of the People." The term is used by the Navajos to refer to what is now northwestern New Mexico.

drypaintings Also called sandpaintings, these images are made with dry pigments such as sand and corn pollen by a helper, under the supervision of a singer, for use in some of the curative Navajo ceremonies. Drypaintings range in size from less than 1 foot to more than 20 feet in diameter. After the ritual, the drypainting (usually of a sacred figure or symbol) is destroyed.

hogan A cone- or dome-shaped dwelling with a frame made of logs and bark and covered with a thick coat of mud. Navajo families lived in hogans that usually measured between 20 and 30 feet in diameter.

hozho The Navajo word meaning beauty, happiness, harmony, and goodness. It summarizes the basic goal and ultimate value of the Navajo world.

Indian Claims Commission (ICC) A temporary federal court created by an act of Congress in 1946 to hear and rule on claims brought by Indians against the United States. These claims stemmed from unfulfilled treaty terms, such as nonpayment for land sold by the Indians.

Indian Reorganization Act (IRA) The 1934 federal law that ended the policy of allotting plots of land to individuals and provided for political and economic development of reservation communities. Self-government was permitted, and tribes wrote their own constitutions for that purpose.

kinaalda The four-day ceremony conducted for a Navajo girl when she reaches puberty. During the kinaalda, female elders instruct the girl in what her duties and responsibilities as a Navajo woman will be.

linguistics The study of the nature, structure, and history of human speech and languages.

Long Walk The grueling 250-mile journey of more than 8,000 Navajos to the Bosque Redondo area in northeastern New Mexico Territory in 1863–64. The U.S. Army compelled the Navajos to leave their homeland and relocate at Bosque Redondo after conquering them in battle. The Navajos were allowed to return to their homeland five years later according to the terms of their 1868 treaty with the federal government.

matrilineal descent A principle of descent by which kinship is traced through female ancestors; the basis for the Navajos' clan membership.

mission A ministry commissioned by a religious organization to promote its faith or carry on humanitarian work.

Native American Church A religious organization whose practices combine elements of Christianity with rituals of traditional Indian relgions. Many of these rituals involve the consumption of the hallucinogenic peyote cactus.

origin story A sacred narrative that the people of a society believe explains the origin of the world, their own institutions, and their distinctive culture.

peyote A cactus native to the southwestern United States and northern Mexico. The buttons of the cactus are sometimes eaten as part of Indian religious ceremonies.

reservation A tract of land set aside by treaty for the occupation and use of Indians; also called a reserve, in Canada. Some reservations were for an entire tribe; many others were for several tribes of unaffiliated Indians.

termination The policy that sought to end the federal government's financial responsibilities to tribes and gradually to withdraw its special protection of reservation lands. The goal of this policy was to have individual states assume these responsibilities for the Indians who resided within their boundaries. It was thought that termination policy would encourage the integration of Indians into mainstream American society.

tribe A community or group of communities that occupy a common territory and are related by bonds of kinship, language, and shared traditions.

INDEX

AFL-CIO, 97
Agriculture, 22, 36, 49, 94
Ahkeah, Sam, 82, 83, 87
Air pollution, 95
Alaska, 18
Albuquerque, New Mexico, 55
American Indian Movement (AIM), 100
American settlers, 37, 39, 45
Anasazi Indians, 32, 50
Apache Indians, 18
Apaches de Nabajó, 18
Arizona, 13, 20, 35, 39, 43, 46, 50, 52, 55, 62, 85, 86, 90, 97
Arizona Public Service Company, 94
Arizona State University, 100
Arizona, University of, 98
Ashiihi clan, 29
Asia, 18
Athapaska Lake, 18
Athapuscan language, 18
Atlantic Ocean, 25

Bacone High School, 93
Bailey, F. Lee, 100
Bancroft, George, 57
Barboncito, 40, 44, 45, 46, 47, 103
Bardony, Todachene, 57
Bega, Becenti, 57
Bega, Hosteen Begoiden, 57
Bekis, Dugal Chee, 56
Bering Strait, 18
BIA schools. *See* Education
Billy, Bahe, 98
Black Horse, 56
Black Mesa, 43, 94
Blanca Peak (Dawn or White Shell Mountains), 14
Blankets, 31, 53
Blessingway rite, 33–34, 80
Boarding schools. *See* Education
Borrego Pass School, 90
Bosque Redondo, 41, 43, 49, 51
Boulder Dam, 62, 63
Brigham City, Utah, 86

Brigham Young University, 91
Brooks, William T. H., 40
Brown, Vlassis and Bain, 97
Bureau of Indian Affairs (BIA), 45, 52, 55, 56, 61, 62, 73, 85, 86, 89

Cahcheschillige, Deshna, 57
Calhoun, John, 39
California, 37, 39, 93, 94
Canada, 18
Canyon de Chelly, 42, 43, 98
Carleton, James, 40–44, 45
Carlisle, Pennsylvania, 55
Carlisle Indian Industrial School, 55
Carson, Kit, 42
Cattle, 24, 47, 50–51, 60
Ceremonies, 32–35, 76–80, 103
Changing Woman, 15, 16, 32
Chantways, 32
Chaves, Manuel, 40
Chevrolet, 98
Child Born of Water, 15–17
China, 22
Christianity, 23, 36, 42. *See also* Methodists, Presbyterians, Roman Catholic church
Christian Reformed Church, 54
Chuska, Arizona, 89
Chuska Mountains, 39
Civil War, 41, 42, 45
College. *See* Education
Collier, John, 62–63, 64, 73
Colorado, 22, 37, 39, 86
Colorado Plateau, 22
Colorado River, 62, 63, 98
Columbus, Christopher, 22, 25
Comanche Indians, 45
Confederacy, 41
Contract Schools. *See* Education
Corn, 16, 29, 36
Court system, 60, 87
Cradleboards, 27

Craftwork, 21, 53, 94. *See also* Blankets, Jewelry, Rugs, Silversmiths, Turquoise

Davis, Don, 98
Department of the Interior, 45
Diné, 22
Dinebeiina Nahiilna be Agitahe (DNA), 92–93, 100
Dinétah, 22, 103
Dodge, Chee, 56, 57, 73, 74
Drypainting, 34–35

Economy, 53, 84, 86, 93, 94, 97, 101
Education, 46, 49, 54–56, 73, 85–86, 89–91, 97
Elk, 20
Enemyway ceremony, 80
English language, 20, 53, 55, 86, 87, 90
Europeans, 22, 23, 31, 36
Exxon, 97

Fairchild Semiconductor, 95, 100
Family life
   child raising, 27–28, 30
   marriage, 28–29
Farming. *See* Agriculture
Farmington, New Mexico, 55
Federal Emergency Relief Administration, 64
First Man, 14
First Woman, 14
Flagstaff, Arizona, 85
Fort Defiance, 40, 42, 43, 49, 54, 55–56, 57
Fort Fauntleroy, 40
Fort Sumner, 41, 43, 44, 45, 49, 103
Fort Wingate, 43
Four Corners, 86
Four Corners Power Plant, 94
Four sacred mountains, 14, 15, 47
Fourth world, 14

Franciscans, 54
Fryer, E. Reesman, 73

Gallup, New Mexico, 55, 85
Ganado, Arizona, 54, 91
Ganado, College of, 91
Ganado Mission School, 54
Ganado Mucho, 40, 44
Gaston, Charity, 49
General Dynamics
　Corporation, 95
Germans, 80
Gobernador Knob, 14
Goldwater, Barry, 100
Grand Canyon, 102
Grants, New Mexico, 17, 97
Great Depression, 62
Guadalupe Hidalgo, Treaty
　of, 39
Guam, 79

Harrisburg, Pennsylvania, 97
Haskell Institute, 55
Haskie, Leonard, 103
History. See Navajos
　(origins)
Hogan. See Housing
Holy People, 14, 15, 32, 36
Home Improvement
　Training, 93
Hoover, Herbert, 62
Hoover Dam, 62
Hopi Indian Agency, 56
Hopi Indians, 22, 50, 55, 91,
　96, 100, 101
Horses, 24, 35, 50–51, 64
Housing, 21, 28, 97
Hozho, 32, 33, 80
Hubbell, Lorenzo, 53, 54
Huerfano Mountain, 14
Hughes Aircraft, 93
Hunter, John, 60
Hupa Indians, 18

Indian Claims Commission
　(ICC), 82
Indian Reorganization Act
　(IRA), 64–65
Indian Territory, 45, 46
Intermountain School, 86
Isabella I, 22

Italians, 80
Iwo Jima, 79

Japanese, 79
Jemez Pueblo, 36
Jesus, Hosteen Yazzie, 57
Jewelry, 53, 54
Johnson, Lyndon B., 92
Johnston, Phillip, 79
Jones, Paul, 87

Keam, Thomas, 53
Keams Canyon, 53, 55
Kinaalda, 15, 34
Kinyaa'aanii clan, 29
KTNN-Radio, 102

La Plata Mountain (Obsidian
　Mountain), 14
Lawrence, Kansas, 55
Legal Aid Service, 92
Leupp, Arizona, 60
Leupp Jurisdiction, 56
Littell, Norman, 82, 97
Livestock reduction, 50–52,
　60–64, 73–74, 81, 103
Long Walk, 43, 49, 50, 53,
　77, 103
Low Mountain, Arizona, 100

MacDonald, Peter, 93–94,
　96, 97, 98, 99, 100, 101,
　102, 103
Manuelito, 40, 44
Manufacturing, 95
Many Farms, Arizona, 89,
　91
Martin, Robert, 57
Meritt, A. B., 60
Mescalero Apache Indians,
　41, 42
Methodists, 54
Mexican War (1846–48), 37,
　39
Mexico, 22, 37, 39, 54
Midwest Refining Company,
　56
Mining, 41, 86, 94–95, 97
Missionaries, 23–24, 54–55
Mission schools, 54–55, 85.
　See also Education
Mississippi River, 41

Mitchell, Charlie, 56
Moenkopi, 54
Monster Slayer, 15–17, 32
Monument Valley, 98
Moore, J. B., 53
Moqui Jurisdiction, 56
Morgan, Jacob, 57, 64, 83
Mormons, 54
Mott, Harold, 97
Mount Taylor (Blue Bead or
　Turquoise Mountain), 14

Nabajó, 18–19
Nakei, Raymond, 93, 94, 96,
　97, 98, 100
Narbona, 39–40
Native American Church,
　75, 76. See also Peyote
Navajo, New Mexico, 98
Navajo Agricultural
　Products Industry
　(NAPI), 98. See also
　Agriculture
Navajo Codetalkers, 79–81,
　93
Navajo Community College
　(NCC), 91. See also
　Education
Navajo Curriculum Center,
　90
Navajo Divison of
　Education, 97. See also
　Education
Navajo Forest Products
　Industry (NFPI), 87, 98
Navajo-Hopi Rehabilitation
　Act, 83
Navajo Housing Authority
　97, 100. See also Housing
Navajo Indian Irrigation
　Project, 98
Navajo Methodist Mission
　School, 55
Navajo Nation, 50, 86, 93,
　103
Navajos
　administrative areas, 56,
　73; clans, 29–30;
　clothing, 21, 28;
　cooperative businesses,
　99; culture, 20–25, 27–37,
　54; employment, 75,

81–82, 94, 97; fishing and hunting, 20, 21, 27, 28; food, 31; government, 56–57, 59, 60, 64, 73, 77, 85, 93, 97; industry, 94; interaction with American military, 37, 39–44; interaction with other tribes. *See* Hopis, Pueblos; involvement in World War II, 79–82; joint-use land, 96–97, 100–101; language, 18–20; legal representation, 82–83, 92, 97; marriage. *See* Family life; natural resources, 94–95, 97, 98; origins (archaeological), 18–21, (traditional), 13–18; police force, 60, 76, 103; politics, 35, 97, 99, 100, 101–102; population, 89; size (tribe), 13, 89; spiritual beliefs, 21, 31–32, 75

Navajo Times, 87, 102

Navajo Tribal Council, 56, 57, 59–60, 73, 76–77, 83, 86, 91, 94, 103

Navajo Tribal Utilities Authority (NTUA), 87

Neighborhood Youth Corps, 93

Nevada, 37, 39

New Deal, 63

New Mexico, 13, 14, 18, 22, 35, 36, 37, 39, 40, 41, 42, 46, 55, 56, 62, 63, 85, 86, 90, 94, 97, 98

New Spain, 23, 25

Nez, Hosteen, 57

Nidah', 32–33

North America, 18, 20, 22, 37, 82

Office of Economic Opportunity (OEO), 92

Office of Navajo Economic Opportunity (ONEO), 92, 93, 94

Ohio, 20

Oil, 56, 59, 86, 94, 97

Oklahoma, 45, 93

Oklahoma, University of, 93

Page, Arizona, 94

Peabody Coal Company, 94

Pearl Harbor, Hawaii, 79

Pecos River, 41, 43, 45

Peyote, 76

Phoenix, Arizona, 55, 81, 97, 100

Pinon, Arizona, 99

Pinon Co-op, 99

Platero, Utah, 91

Popay, 36

Presbyterians, 54

Provo, Utah, 91

Pueblo Bonito Jurisdiction, 56

Pueblos Indians, 22, 23, 28, 35, 36, 50, 53, 62

Railroads, 47, 75

Ramah School, 90

Rehoboth, 55

Rehoboth Mission School, 55

Religion. *See* Navajos (spiritual beliefs)

Relocation policies, 41–47, 49

Reservations, 41, 45–47, 50, 56

Rio Grande, 22, 35

Riordan, Dennis, 52

Riverside, California, 86

Rock Point School, 90

Roessel, Robert, 90

Roman Catholic church, 23, 36, 54

Roosevelt, Franklin D., 62

Rough Rock Demonstration School, 90

Rugs, 13, 31, 53

St. Michaels Mission School, 54

San Francisco Peak (Abalone Shell Mountain), 14

San Juan Jurisdiction, 56, 57

San Juan Pueblo, 36

San Juan River, 94, 98

Sanostee, New Mexico, 103

Santa Fe, New Mexico, 55

Santa Fe railroad, 53

Self-determination policy, 93, 98, 99

Sheep raising, 24, 29, 30–31, 35, 46, 50–51, 74, 81, 94

Sherman, William Tecumseh, 45, 46

Sherman Institute, 86

Shipley, Dana K., 50, 55–56

Shiprock, New Mexico, 55, 56, 57, 64, 91

Shiprock Mountain, 18

Sidney, Ivan, 101

Silversmiths, 53–54

Snakes, 32

Soil erosion, 51–52, 61–62, 63, 73

South America, 18, 22

Southern Jurisdiction, 56, 57

Southwest, 18, 21, 22, 28, 31, 39, 50, 51, 59

Spanish, 18, 22–25, 27, 30, 35, 36, 37

Spider Woman, 16–17, 18

Sun, 15, 17, 18

Taos, New Mexico, 42

Tappa, Samuel F., 45

Tarawa, 79

Teec Nos Poz, Arizona, 93

Termination policy, 82–84

Texas, Republic of, 37

Three Mile Island, 97

Tl'izilani clan, 29

Toadlena, New Mexico, 57

To'aheedliinii clan, 29

Todichi'iinii clan, 29

Tohatchi, 55

Tourism, 84, 94, 95, 98

Toyei, Arizona, 89

Trading posts, 43–54, 84, 99

Tsaile, Arizona, 91

Tuba City, Arizona, 54, 89, 98

Turquoise, 54

Union, 41

United Presbyterian church, 91

United States, 20, 22, 37, 39, 40, 46, 53, 55, 62, 77, 79, 89

U.S. Army, 40, 41, 45
U.S. Congress, 45, 82, 85
U.S. Department of Housing and Urban Development (HUD), 97
U.S. government, 39, 46, 49, 86
U.S. Indian Peace Commission, 45
U.S. Marine Corps, 79, 93
U.S. Senate Committee on Indian Affairs, 74
U.S. Senate Select Committee on Indian Affairs, 102
U.S. Women's Army Corps, Uranium, 86, 94, 97–98

Usahelin, Hosteen, 57
Utah, 13, 37, 39, 50, 54, 85, 86
Utah Mining and Manufacturing, 94
Utes Indians, 35, 42

Values, 14, 27, 31, 34, 64
Vanadium Corporation, 86
Vlassis, George, 97

Washington, John, 39
Washington, D.C., 52, 60, 82, 92
Watchman, Louis, 57

Water rights, 98
Weavers, 13, 31, 34, 53
Western Jurisdiction, 56
Window Rock, Arizona, 73, 83, 102
Women
    marriage, 28–29;
    role in family, 30
World War II, 77, 79, 84, 86, 93

Zagenitzo, 57
Zah, Peterson, 100–101
Zarcilla Largo, 40
Zeh, William, 61
Zuni Indians, 50

PICTURE CREDITS

American Museum of Natural History, courtesy Department of Library Services, (negative #34010D) page 23, (negative #2A 3634) page 34, (negative #K12638) page 70, (negative #K13015) pages 70–71, (negative #K12640) page 71, (negative #K12894) page 72 (above); AP/Wide World, pages 77, 78, 91, 93, 101; The Bettman Archive, page 38; Nicholas Brown, Museum of New Mexico, page 42; Bureau of Indian Affairs/Milton Snow Collection at Navajo Tribal Museum, Window Rock, AZ, pages 58, 76; Culver Pictures, pages 52, 62; Richard Erodes/Taurus Photos, pages 87, 92, 95, 102; Eric Kroll/Taurus Photos, page 88; 1981 Laura Gilpen Collection Amon Carter Museum, Fort Worth, TX, pages 20, 26, 54, 86; Michael Latil Photography, courtesy Smithsonian Institution, (catalog #4202579) cover, (catalog #362001) page 65, (catalog #404068) page 66, (catalog #422580) page 67, (above) (catalog #362.031) page 67 (below), (catalog #361.525) page 68 (above), (catalog #165466) page 68 (below), (catalog #404082) pages 68–69, (catalog #361.982) page 69; Library, Academy of Natural Sciences of Philadelphia, MS. Coll. 146 #44 Kern, page 41; Library of Congress, pages 15, 19, 29, 30, 31, 35, 57; Museum of the American Indian. Heye Foundation, page 72 (below); National Archives, (photo #87-964) page 46; Navajo Tribal Museum, Window Rock, AZ, pages 61, 74, 75; Photos courtesy of Native American Painting Reference Library, Private Collection, frontispiece, page 16; L. L. Rhodes/Taurus Photos, page 25; Smithsonian Institute, pages 33, 47, 48; United States Department of the Interior, National Park Service, page 24; UPI/Bettman Newsphotos, pages 36, 43, 63, 80, 81, 83, 84, 99, 100.

Maps (pages 44, 51, 96) by Gary Tong.

PETER IVERSON is a professor of history at Arizona State University and is the author of several books, including two on Navajo history: *The Navajos: A Critical Bibliography* (1976) and *The Navajo Nation* (1983). He received a B.A. in history from Carleton College and M.A. and Ph.D. degrees from the University of Wisconsin. He has received fellowships from the National Endowment for the Humanities, the W. K. Kellogg Foundation, and the D'Arcy McNickle Center for the History of the American Indian at the Newberry Library in Chicago. In 1984 the Navajo Nation awarded Dr. Iverson the Chief Manuelito Appreciation Award for his contributions to Navajo education, including three years as a teacher at Navajo Community College.

FRANK W. PORTER III, general editor of INDIANS OF NORTH AMERICA, is director of the Chelsea House Foundation for American Indian Studies. He holds a B.A., M.A., and Ph.D. from the University of Maryland. He has done extensive research concerning the Indians of Maryland and Delaware and is the author of numerous articles on their history, archaeology, geography, and ethnography. He was formerly director of the Maryland Commission on Indian Affairs and American Indian Research and Resource Institute, Gettysburg, Pennsylvania, and he has received grants from the Delaware Humanities Forum, the Maryland Committee for the Humanities, the Ford Foundation, and the National Endowment for the Humanities, among others. Dr. Porter is the author of *The Bureau of Indian Affairs* in the Chelsea House KNOW YOUR GOVERNMENT series.